Flavors of
the Middle East

Flavors of
the Middle East

spiced and aromatic feasts from the ancient lands

Ghillie Başan

photography by Steve Painter

RYLAND PETERS & SMALL
LONDON • NEW YORK

DESIGN, PHOTOGRAPHY AND
PROP STYLING Steve Painter
EDITORS Nathan Joyce and
Rebecca Woods
PRODUCTION MANAGER Gordana
Simakovic
ART DIRECTOR Leslie Harrington
EDITORIAL DIRECTOR Julia Charles

FOOD STYLIST Lucy McKelvie
FOOD STYLIST'S ASSISTANT Ellie Jarvis
INDEXER Hilary Bird

First published in 2014 by
Ryland Peters & Small
20–21 Jockey's Fields
London WC1R 4BW
and
519 Broadway, 5th Floor
New York, NY 10012

www.rylandpeters.com

10 9 8 7 6 5 4 3 2 1

Text © Ghillie Basan 2014
Design and photographs ©
Ryland Peters & Small 2014

Printed in China

UK ISBN: 978-1-84975-492-7
US ISBN: 978-1-84975-537-5

A CIP record for this book is available from
the British Library.

US Library of Congress CIP data has been
applied for.

NOTES
· All spoon measurements are level unless
otherwise specified.
· All eggs are medium (UK) or large (US),
unless otherwise specified. Uncooked or
partially cooked eggs should not be served
to the very old, frail, young children,
pregnant women or those with
compromised immune systems.
· When a recipe calls for the grated zest of
citrus fruit, buy unwaxed fruit and wash
well before using. If you can only find
treated fruit, scrub well in warm soapy
water before use.

· Ovens should be preheated to the specified
temperatures. We recommend using an oven
thermometer. If using a fan-assisted oven,
adjust temperatures according to the
manufacturer's instructions.
· To sterilize preserving jars, wash them in
hot, soapy water and rinse in boiling water.
Place in a large saucepan and cover with hot
water. With the saucepan lid on, bring the
water to a boil and continue boiling for
15 minutes. Turn off the heat and leave the
jars in the hot water until just before they
are to be filled. Invert the jars onto a clean
tea/dish towel to dry. Sterilize the lids for
5 minutes, by boiling or according to the
manufacturer's instructions. Jars should be
filled and sealed while they are still hot.

contents

Introduction

If Africa is the birthplace of the human species and the Middle East is considered the birthplace of civilization, then it could also be argued that the latter is the birthplace of sophisticated food. Archaeological records show that some of the earliest organized societies lived in the valley of the River Nile and in the Fertile Crescent of Mesopotamia (ancient Iraq), also known as the 'Cradle of Civilization'. In this land, the meat of wild and domestic animals were roasted whole over open fires; wheat, barley and vegetables were cultivated; honey and date juice were used as natural sweeteners, and milk was turned into cheese and butter. The cooking methods and recipes would have been simple — inspiration from the trade in spices and flavourings and sophistication from the lavish court cuisine of Persia and Baghdad came later — but the foundations were there and, in some rural communities today, little has changed.

The first wave of spices and other culinary articles of trade to influence the region came with the seafaring Phoenicians to the shores of the eastern Mediterranean, until Alexander the Great conquered their seaports and set up his own entrepôt, Alexandria, at the mouth of the Nile. Under Alexander the Great, the Greeks' territory encompassed most of Asia Minor, the Middle East, Persia and northwest India and it was at this time that aubergines/eggplants and lemons are thought to have come into the Middle East from India. At this point in time, the refined ingredients of the Persian court, such as saffron, pomegranates and pistachios, spread into the Mediterranean regions.

When the Persians re-established themselves as an Empire after the death of Alexander the Great, they wielded a strong culinary influence from Greece to India and Russia to Egypt with the ancient silk routes passing through the northern region and the trade routes to the south. The Romans took control of the sea routes and the Han emperors regulated the silk routes, displacing the Mongol and pastoral tribes of Central Asia; these tribes were forced to move westwards and invade new territories, which ultimately led to the severing of the overland routes and played a part in the fall of the great Roman Empire.

As the Roman Empire had controlled the whole of the Mediterranean world, this was divided into two empires — the eastern half (the Levant, Egypt and Asia Minor) became the Byzantine Empire, while the Persians, under the Sassanid dynasty, continued to rule what is now Iran and their eastern territories including Afghanistan and Pakistan. Only the nomads of the desert and the frankincense kingdoms of Saudi Arabia remained independent. This was a time of lavish feasts for both the Byzantine and Sassanid courts with a fascinating mix of culinary traditions and philosophies, inspired by the territories they controlled. Some of the Persian banquets included the stuffed and roasted meat of camels, water buffaloes, donkeys and gazelles; meat was often marinated in spices and yogurt, or combined with fruit in stews; nuts were ground to thicken sauces or fill pastries; and fruit was preserved in jams and conserves — traditions that are still in evidence today.

The spread of Islam changed the face of the Middle East forever more. Following the death of the Prophet Mohammed in AD 632, the Arabs of the Arabian Peninsula conquered Greater Syria and Persia, spreading Islam and its culinary restrictions on the slaughtering of animals and the consumption of alcohol wherever they went, until their Empire stretched right across Asia and North Africa and into Sicily and Spain. The Golden Age of Islam began in the late 8th century when Arab ships sailed to China for silk and porcelain, to the East Indies for spices, and to East Africa for ivory and gold. With Mecca as its religious centre and Baghdad as its capital, it was a time of cultural and culinary awakening, and the banquets held at the courts of the Caliphs of Baghdad were legendary for their extravagance, inspired by the gastronomical beliefs and food vocabulary they had adopted from the Persians.

The next significant wave of culinary influence in the Middle East came with the Turks, fierce tribal warriors who had moved westwards through Central Asia with their own gastronomical traditions of skewered and preserved meat, among other creations including a unique type of noodle dough. The Seljuk Turks settled in Konya (in the now Central Anatolia region of Turkey) and ruled Greater Syria for most of the 12th century, but the most significant cultural, social and culinary development in the region started with a tribal chief's son named Osman, who converted to Islam and established the Ottoman Empire, which determined the destiny of the Middle East, North Africa and the Balkans for the next five centuries.

By the middle of the 15th century, Constantinople (now known as Istanbul) was the capital of the Empire and the Topkapı Palace became the centre of all indulgent and sophisticated culinary activity, where they adopted and adapted dishes from the different regions they conquered. The palace contained specialist pastry chefs, dessert chefs, and even chefs who only made meatballs or rice pilafs. There were reputed to be over 200 dishes prepared with aubergines/eggplants and, under the reign of Suleyman the Magnificent, the industrious chefs of the Palace kitchens created a wide range of sensuously named dishes, including one which translates as 'ladies' thighs'.

In the 16th century, the Ottomans came to an agreement with the seafaring Spaniards that the ships transporting goods from the New World would stop at the North African coast en route to Spain. This way the goods, such as chillies/chiles, corn and tomatoes, which had never before been seen or used in the Middle East,

would reach Constantinople from Egypt and be incorporated into the cuisine and distributed to the far-reaching corners of the Empire. By the time the Ottoman Empire collapsed with the defeat of Turkey in the First World War, it had established such a vast culinary influence that its glorious legacy is still evident on the tables of Morocco, the Middle East, Turkey and the Balkans.

The territories of the Ottoman Empire were divided up after the First World War – the French controlled Syria and Lebanon; the British administered Palestine, Transjordan, Iraq and Egypt; and the Republic of Turkey was declared. After the Second World War, the British terminated the mandate of Palestine and the United Nations divided it into Arab and Jewish states and, over time, the other countries of the region gained their own independence. The Middle East today is a vaguely defined area where three continents of the world meet. When it comes to food, the modern boundaries are fairly fluid

and irrelevant as the region's history has provided so many reasons for culinary traditions and dishes to cross over and appear in different countries.

The geographical differences between all of these countries has an impact on the culinary traditions of the region. There are large, empty deserts with the occasional date palm oasis; long coastlines and ferocious rivers; high, rugged mountains; lush hillsides and valleys; marshlands, salt lakes, large freshwater lakes, inland seas and the Dead Sea; and miles and miles of arid or fertile, flat plains. Countries, like Iran, Turkey and Morocco are blessed with a generous share of varied terrain, lush pastures and both fresh and salt waters, whereas Iraq has comparatively little coastline and Libya is largely desert.

Every village, valley and hillside tell a story: the Pyramids of Egypt; the tomb of the Virgin Mary; the desert where John the Baptist survived off locusts; the Roman amphitheatres and Crusaders' castles; the Bedouin camps and troglodyte dwellings; and the Christian and Byzantine churches, Jewish synagogues and magnificent mosques. The region has witnessed the civilizations of Mesopotamians, Phoenicians, Assyrians, Babylonians, Persians, Armenians, Cappadocians, Kurds, Arabs, Turks, Muslims, Jews and Christians, all of whom have one thing in common — the food of the land they inhabited.

The combination of a unifying history and shared ingredients has developed into one Middle Eastern culinary tradition with four predominant roots: the sophisticated, Indian-influenced Persian cuisine and the introduction of rice dishes; the renowned Arab cuisine of the Fertile Crescent — Syria, Lebanon, and Jordan — with the richest variety of vegetable dishes; the wide-ranging cuisine of the Ottoman Empire, which influenced countries beyond the boundaries of the Middle East; and the distinctive culinary traditions of North Africa, some of which can be linked all the way back to the ancient cooking styles of Persia. A feast for the eyes and the palate, the flavours of the Middle East are worth exploring and enjoying while you reflect on the fact that you are tasting some of the earliest, most sophisticated dishes of human civilization!

basic recipes

Dukkah

Derived from the Arabic word for 'to pound', dukkah is a popular and versatile Middle Eastern spice mix. The ingredients vary from region to region and family to family but a typical mix will include sesame seeds, coriander and cumin seeds, roasted hazelnuts or pistachios and salt. Sometimes dried mint, dried chilli/chile or roasted chickpeas are added. The key to making a traditional dukkah is to crush the spices, using a pestle and mortar, rather than grind them to a powder, as you are looking for texture as well as flavour. The mixture is then bound with a little olive oil and bread is dipped into it for breakfast or a snack — a popular street snack in Egypt and Jordan where you can buy the dukkah spice mix in paper cones and chunks of bread to dip in it. The mixture is also used as a coating for stir-fried or grilled strips of chicken, lamb or fish and, combined with olive oil and lemon juice, it can be used as a dressing for salads. It is easy to make your own dukkah at home; sprinkle it over grilled meat, roasted vegetables, pulse/bean dishes, or a crunchy carrot and cabbage salad.

4 tablespoons hazelnuts

2 tablespoons sesame seeds

1 tablespoon coriander seeds

1 tablespoon cumin seeds

1 tablespoon fennel seeds

2 teaspoons fine chilli/hot red pepper flakes

2 teaspoons dried mint

1–2 teaspoons sea salt

sterilized jar

Makes 6 tablespoons

Dry roast the hazelnuts in a heavy based pan until they emit a nutty aroma. Rub off any loose skins and, using a pestle and mortar, crush the nuts lightly. Dry roast the sesame, coriander, cumin and fennel seeds, along with the chilli/hot red pepper flakes, until they emit a nutty aroma. Add them to the hazelnuts. Crush the mixture lightly so that it is blended but uneven in texture — with some nuts and seeds almost a powder.

Stir in the mint and sea salt to taste and spoon the mixture into a sterilized, airtight jar. Keep the jar in a cupboard, away from direct sunlight, for 4–6 weeks.

Samna
(clarified butter)

Traditionally, butter was made in a churn fashioned from the tanned skin of a whole goat. Partially filled with milk and tied at the ends, the skin was suspended by four ropes, which were secured to the legs of the skin. The woman of the household would then sit beside the skin and jerk it to and fro until the milk was churned — an age-old tradition that is still utilized in the remote rural villages and by the Bedouin in their temporary camps. Butter was lavishly used in the cooking of the Medieval and Ottoman periods and the Syrian cities, Aleppo and Hama, were well known for the quality of their delicious, creamy butter and the clarified version, 'samna' or 'samneh'. Depending on where you are in the Middle East, butter can be made from the milk of sheep, goats, cows, camels or buffaloes and it can have quite a strong rancid smell and taste, which villagers often prefer, such as the Moroccan aged and flavoured butter, 'smen'. Clarifying butter is the best method of preserving it as well as producing a cooking fat with a delicious nutty flavour and aroma, which is imparted to both sweet and savoury dishes. It is widely used in Asian cuisine, where it is known as 'ghee'.

450 g/1 lb. butter

muslin/cheesecloth

sterilized container or jar

Makes 350 g/12 oz.

To make samna or ghee at home, simply cut a block of butter (450 g/1 lb. will reduce to approximately 350 g/12 oz.) into chunks. Put the chunks into a heavy based pan and melt them gently over a low heat so that they do not brown. Allow the melted butter to froth gently until the fat is as transparent as a teardrop. Then take it off the heat and leave it to settle before straining it through a piece of muslin/cheesecloth (to remove the impurities) into a clean container. Discard any milky solids at the bottom of the pan. Seal the container and store the samna in a cool place or in the refrigerator for at least 6 months to use in place of butter or oil whenever you like.

Harissa

This is a fiery paste from North Africa made with dried or roasted red chillies/chiles and spices. It has a very versatile nature as it can be used as a condiment with grilled or roasted ingredients and with fried or boiled eggs; as a marinade by adding more oil; as the base of a sauce or dip (just stir a little into thick yogurt); as a flavouring in any type of soup, stew or grain dish. It enhances a dish with its depth of flavour and chilli/chile kick! Called 'harissa' in Morocco and other parts of North Africa, it is also known as a 'Moroccan paste' or simply a 'chilli/chile paste' in other regions and is not to be confused with the Middle Eastern one-pot 'harissa', a dish of bulgur and lamb. Jars and tubes of ready-prepared harissa are available in Middle Eastern stores, as well as some supermarkets, but it's easy to make a small quantity at home; a little goes a long way.

8 dried long red chillies/chiles

2 teaspoons cumin seeds

2 teaspoons coriander seeds

3–4 garlic cloves, chopped

1–2 teaspoons sea salt

4 tablespoons olive oil

sterilized jar

Makes 3 tablespoons

Put the chillies/chiles in a bowl and pour over enough warm water to cover them. Leave them to soak for at least 6 hours or overnight so that they soften. Dry roast the cumin and coriander seeds and grind them to a powder in a pestle and mortar.

Drain the chillies/chiles, cut off the stalks and squeeze out most of the seeds. Discard the stalks and seeds, then roughly chop them. Using a pestle and mortar, pound the chillies/chiles with the garlic and salt to form a thick, smooth paste — this takes a while but it is well worth the effort.

Beat in the ground spices and pound the paste again. Add half the olive oil and, at this stage, you can add other ingredients of your choice such as fresh or dried mint or oregano, finely chopped fresh coriander/cilantro, or finely chopped dried orange peel.

Spoon the mixture into a sterilized jar and pour over the rest of the oil. Seal the jar and store it in a cool place or in the refrigerator for 1-2 months and just use a little when you need it.

Zhug

Fiery chilli/chile, cardamom and garlic flavours are characteristic of Yemeni cooking and they are all concentrated in the traditional spice paste, zhug (zhoug). Usually it is served with bread and eaten as a snack or appetizer but zhug is also used as a condiment for a variety of grilled and roasted dishes, or combined with puréed tomatoes and fresh coriander/cilantro and served as a mezze dish. Popular in Yemen, Oman, the United Arab Emirates and Saudi Arabia, it is a versatile chilli/chile paste like harissa.

8 dried long red chillies/chiles

4 garlic cloves, roughly chopped

1 teaspoon sea salt

seeds of 4–6 cardamom pods

1 teaspoon caraway seeds

½ teaspoon black peppercorns

1 small bunch fresh flat-leaf parsley, finely chopped

a small bunch of fresh coriander/cilantro, finely chopped

3–4 tablespoons olive or sunflower oil

sterilized jar

Makes 4–5 tablespoons

Put the chillies/chiles in a bowl and pour over enough warm water to cover them. Leave them to soak for at least 6 hours or overnight so that they soften. Drain them, cut off the stalks and squeeze out the seeds. Discard the stalks and seeds and then roughly chop them.

Using a pestle and mortar, pound the chillies/chiles with the garlic and salt to form a thick, smooth paste. Add the cardamom and caraway seeds and the peppercorns. Pound them with the chilli/chile paste — you want to break up the seeds and peppercorns but they don't have to be perfectly ground as a little bit of texture is good. Beat in the parsley and coriander/cilantro and bind the mixture with most of the oil.

Spoon the spice paste into a sterilized jar, drizzle the rest of the oil over the top and keep it in a cool place or in the refrigerator, for 3–4 weeks. When serving as a condiment or a dip for bread, mix the layer of oil into the zhug and garnish with finely chopped flat-leaf parsley.

Lemons preserved in salt

Salt is a natural preserver and has been since ancient times – the Egyptians used it to preserve mummies and the Hebrews dipped bread in salt to symbolize God's covenant with Israel – Jews still do this on the Sabbath. Loyalty and friendship have traditionally been sealed with salt and, in Christianity, salt is associated with truth, wisdom and a long life. Both Muslims and Jews believe that salt protects against the evil eye and, in some communities, the excess salt from a too liberal sprinkling must be tossed over the left shoulder with a blessing for good luck. Some Jews rub salt over newborn babies for good luck, while others still believe in the medieval law that a man must only handle salt with the middle two fingers – his children will die if he uses his thumb, the family will become poor if he uses his little finger, and he will become a murderer if he uses his index finger. When it comes to food, though, salt is a saviour – a miraculous preserver of meat, fish, vegetables and fruit – and perhaps the best example of all are the ubiquitous lemons preserved in salt, 'l'hamd markad'. Most commonly associated with North Africa, particularly Moroccan tagines, preserved lemons are used throughout the Middle East. Sometimes, they are preserved in brine, vinegar or oil, but the flavour of the salted variety is supreme and, generally, it is only the rind, finely chopped or sliced, that is used to enhance salads, vegetable dishes and some roasted and grilled dishes. Preserved lemons are readily available in Middle Eastern stores but they are also very easy and satisfying to make at home.

8 organic, unwaxed lemons

roughly 8 tablespoons/½ cup sea salt

freshly squeezed juice of 3–4 unwaxed lemons

large sterilized jar

Wash and dry the lemons and slice the ends off each one. Stand each lemon on one end and make two vertical cuts three-quarters of the way through them, as if cutting them into quarters but keeping the base intact. Use a spoon to stuff a tablespoon of salt into each lemon and pack them into a large sterilized jar. Store the lemons in a cool place for 3–4 days to soften the skins.

Press the lemons down into the jar, so they are even more tightly packed. Pour the freshly squeezed lemon juice over the salted lemons, until they are completely covered. Seal the jar and store it in a cool place for at least a month. Rinse the salt off the preserved lemons before using as described in the recipes – just the rind, finely chopped or sliced, is used and the flesh is discarded.

Labna

Labna is simply yogurt that has been strained over a period of time so that it is thick and creamy, the consistency of creamy cheese. It is sometimes referred to as 'yogurt cheese'. At home I often prepare labna by straining the yogurt through muslin/cheesecloth suspended over a bowl or the sink. Labna is such a useful thing to have in the refrigerator – by adding herbs, garlic or harissa you have an instant dip; by adding honey, preserved or fresh fruit, roasted nuts or toasted cereals, you have an instant dessert or breakfast. Labna is also used to stuff fruit such as fresh figs or preserved apricots, it is served as a substitute to clotted cream and, if you take the draining one step further by leaving the yogurt suspended for 48 hours, you can mould the labna into little balls, 'labna bi zayt'. Leave them to dry out then drizzle them with olive oil and serve as a mezze dish. Yogurt is an ancient and ubiquitous ingredient throughout the Middle East and it is often served to accompany other dishes and to form the basis of sumptuous mezze dishes.

1 kg/5 cups thick, creamy yogurt

long wooden spoon

I-m/3-ft ⅓ in. string or twine

large piece of muslin/cheesecloth

Makes 500 g/2 cups

To make labna, line a bowl with muslin/cheesecloth, overlapping the sides of the bowl and tip the yogurt into the middle. Pull up the corners of the muslin/cheesecloth and tie each corner over and around the handle of a wooden spoon, or around the tap/faucet in the kitchen sink, and suspend the pouch above the bowl for 4–6 hours. The quantity of yogurt will have reduced by half and you'll end up with a little ball of fluffy, white yogurt cheese, which will keep in the refrigerator for a week.

mezze, salads and soups

2–3 tablespoons olive or argan oil

2 onions, roughly chopped

2 celery stalks, trimmed and diced

2 small carrots, peeled and diced

2–3 garlic cloves, left whole and smashed

2 teaspoons cumin seeds

2 teaspoons coriander seeds

2–3 teaspoons ground turmeric

2 teaspoons sugar

2–3 fresh bay leaves

2–3 whole dried chillies/chiles

1 tablespoon tomato purée/paste

1 litre/4 cups vegetable stock or water

1 x 400-g/14.5-oz. can of chopped tomatoes, drained

1 x 400-g/14.5-oz. can of chickpeas, drained and rinsed

sea salt and freshly ground black pepper

a small bunch of fresh flat-leaf parsley, roughly chopped

a small bunch of fresh coriander/cilantro, roughly chopped

150 g/5 oz. feta, rinsed and drained

1 lemon, cut into quarters, to serve

Serves 4–6

Chickpea and vegetable soup with feta

Chickpeas were first grown in the Levant and ancient Egypt from where they spread throughout the Middle East and to North Africa and India. They were traditionally regarded as a poor man's food and became a staple of the Arab armies as they invaded neighbouring territories, leaving a legacy of chickpeas and many other culinary influences in places like Morocco, Spain and Sicily. Often used as a substitute for potatoes, rice or meat, chickpeas are a great favourite in hearty stews and soups, such as this vegetarian version of the Moroccan lamb and chickpea harira, of which variations can be found throughout the Islamic world.

Heat the oil in the base of a deep, heavy-based saucepan. Stir in the onions, celery and carrots and cook until the onions begin to colour. Add the smashed garlic, cumin and coriander seeds and stir in the turmeric, sugar, bay leaves and chillies/chiles. Add the tomato purée/paste, pour in the stock and bring the liquid to the boil. Reduce the heat, cover with a lid and simmer for 10–15 minutes.

Add the chopped tomatoes and chickpeas and simmer for a further 10 minutes. Season the soup with salt and pepper and add most of the parsley and coriander/cilantro. Crumble the feta over the top, sprinkle with the remaining parsley and coriander/cilantro and serve the soup with wedges of lemon to squeeze over it.

Fish soup with harissa and dried limes

In the Middle East, fish soups are far less common than ones prepared with vegetables, pulses/beans or meat which is surprising given the abundance of fresh and sea water fish in many of the markets. In general, the tradition has been to grill or bake fish and serve it as a main course but there are several fish soups and stews of note; like this one prepared with limes that have been left out to dry in the sun to impart a musty, tangy flavour to the dish. Variations of this soup can be tasted in Oman, Iran, Iraq, the United Arab Emirates and along the North African coast.

2–3 garlic cloves, roughly chopped

40 g/1 ½ oz. fresh ginger, peeled and roughly chopped

sea salt

1–2 tablespoons Samna (page 13), or 1–2 tablespoons olive oil with a knob/pat of butter

2 onions, finely chopped

1–2 teaspoons granulated sugar or honey

1–2 teaspoons ground turmeric

1–2 teaspoons Harissa (page 14)

2–3 dried limes, pierced twice with a skewer

1 x 400 g can/14.5 oz. chopped tomatoes

1 litre/1 quart fish stock or water

900 g/2 lbs. firm, skinned fish fillets (such as sea bass, grouper, turbot, tuna, mackerel or trout), cut into bite-size pieces

freshly ground black pepper

a bunch of fresh coriander/cilantro, finely chopped

Serves 4

Using a pestle and mortar, pound the garlic with the ginger and roughly half a teaspoon of salt to form a thick, almost smooth paste.

Heat the samna, or olive oil and butter in a heavy-based saucepan and stir in the onions for 2–3 minutes to soften them. Add the sugar along with the garlic and ginger paste and cook for about 2 minutes until fragrant. Toss in the turmeric, harissa and dried limes for a minute, then stir in the tomatoes and fish stock. Bring the liquid to the boil, reduce the heat and simmer gently for 15–20 minutes to allow the flavours to mingle.

Season the liquid well with salt and pepper and add the fish chunks. Cover the pan and continue to simmer gently for about 10 minutes, until the fish is cooked. Check the seasoning, stir in half the coriander/cilantro and ladle the soup into bowls. Garnish with the rest of the coriander/cilantro and serve immediately.

Meadow Soup

Yogurt is an ancient and popular ingredient in Middle Eastern cooking, employed in both sweet and savoury dishes, including a variety of traditional soups such as this refreshing mint-flavoured one from Turkey. Often the yogurt is stirred into these soups at the end but, if it is used as part of the cooking liquid, it needs to be stabilized first to prevent it from curdling, unless you are using goat's milk combined with salt. Consumed daily at any time of day or night throughout the Middle East, you can prepare this soup in a variety of traditional ways, such as padding it out with chickpeas, barley, bulgur or rice. Or, you can try an Iranian version with chopped walnuts, a Jewish version prepared with chopped spinach, or an Armenian version thickened with small noodles.

1 tablespoon butter or olive oil

1 large onion, finely chopped

75 g/½ cup long-grain wild rice, well rinsed

1 litre/1 quart chicken or lamb stock

1–2 tablespoons dried mint, plus a little for garnishing

500 ml/2 cups thick, creamy yogurt

sea salt and freshly ground black pepper

warm crusty bread, to serve

Serves 4–6

Heat the butter or oil in a heavy-based pan. Stir in the onion for 2–3 minutes to soften, then toss in the rice. Pour in the stock and bring it to the boil. Reduce the heat, stir in the mint, and simmer gently for about 20 minutes, until the rice is cooked.

Gradually, add the yogurt to the soup, stirring vigorously to make sure it remains smooth and creamy. Keep simmering the soup over a low heat, until it is heated through once more, but don't bring it to the boil. Season well with salt and pepper to taste and garnish the soup with the reserved mint. Serve immediately with chunks of warm, crusty bread.

Spicy lentil soup with zhug and yogurt

First cultivated in Egypt, lentils have long been regarded as a staple of the poor. Derived from the Latin word, 'lentus', meaning 'slow', lentils have stirred up mixed emotions across the Middle East. The ancient Egyptians believed that lentils enlightened the minds of children; the Persians regarded them as a 'cold' food, slowing the metabolism and inducing a calming effect; and the Romans maintained they encouraged a mildness of character, so much so that one Roman general is reputed to have blamed a Persian defeat on the lentils his troops had consumed! Throughout the Middle East, lentils are still regarded as a 'cold' food, a staple of the poor and the nomadic communities, so they are often employed in soups and stews and combined with warming spices, such as cumin, cinnamon and chillies/chiles. Flavoured with the fiery cardamom and garlic paste, Zhug (page 15), from the Yemen, this soup is typical of the region and would traditionally be served with flatbread.

1–2 tablespoons Samna (page 13), or 1–2 tablespoons olive oil with a knob/pat of butter

2 onions, finely chopped

1–2 teaspoons muscovado sugar

2 teaspoons Zhug (page 15)

225 g/1¼ cups brown lentils, washed and rinsed

1.2 litres/5 cups chicken or vegetable stock, or water

sea salt and freshly ground black pepper

roughly 4 tablespoons thick, creamy yogurt

a small bunch of fresh coriander/cilantro, finely chopped

warm crusty bread, to serve

Serves 4–6

Heat the samna, or olive oil and butter in a heavy-based saucepan and stir in the onions with the sugar for 3–4 minutes, until they begin to colour. Stir in the zhug for 1 minute then add the lentils, coating them in the spices. Pour in the stock and bring it to the boil, reduce the heat and simmer for about 20–25 minutes, until the lentils are soft but not mushy.

Season the soup with salt and pepper and ladle it into individual bowls. Drop a small spoonful of yogurt into each bowl of soup and garnish with the coriander/cilantro.

Yogurt: the gift of life

The existence of yogurt as a basic food in the Middle East is as ancient as the earliest nomadic and pastoral tribes who made it from the milk of domesticated goat and camels. Some of the methods employed to curdle the milk are as ancient as these tribes — some nomads use crushed ants' eggs as a yogurt culture, a practice that still continues in some rural communities, but many shepherds and villagers use local herbs, or the branch of a fig tree, as the sap or juices produce a chemical reaction that turns lactose milk into lactic acid.

In medieval manuals, yogurt was referred to as 'Persian milk' and it was used as a food as well as a medicine. The ancestors of the Turks who roamed Central Asia valued yogurt so highly they offered it to the Gods, the Sun and the Moon. In the Middle East today, yogurt is generally known by its Arabic name, 'laban', in Iran it's called 'mast', and in Turkey it is called yoğurt, from which the English word is drawn. Depending on the region, it can be made from the milk of goats, sheep, cows or water buffaloes and, occasionally amongst the Bedouin, it is prepared from camel milk.

In parts of the Middle East, there is a belief that milk is difficult for the stomach to tolerate in its pouring consistency, so it is heated and combined with other ingredients, or it is transformed into yogurt to make it more digestible. The sour taste associated with yogurt is derived from the lactic acid produced by the bacteria during fermentation. In some contexts, the bacteria fuse with yeasts giving the yogurt a slightly fizzy taste, which can be a feature of rural yogurts. Traditionally, yogurt was stored in tin-lined copper urns to keep it cool and fresh for as long as possible, but most villages now have a small shop with refrigeration so commercial yogurt is fairly readily available.

Yogurt is a staple food in the Middle East and it is regarded as a gift of life, the implication being that, if you have nothing else to eat, you could survive by eating yogurt. It is in constant supply throughout the Middle East and the Turks are one of the world's largest consumers. It is like no other single ingredient and is valued as much for its culinary uses as it is for its nutritional and healing qualities. Rich in protein and minerals and containing antibiotic properties, it is as nutritious as it is versatile and forms an integral part of many traditional dishes. It is eaten for breakfast with a drizzle of amber honey; it is enjoyed as a snack dusted with icing/confectioners' sugar; on a hot day, it is diluted with water to make a thirst-quenching drink; it is combined with crushed garlic and added by the spoonful to finish off almost any savoury dish; it is beaten with grated or puréed vegetables to make delectable dips; and it is strained to form a yogurt cheese which can be employed in a variety of tasty savoury and sweet dishes (page 18). A mouthful can also help to put out the fire of an undetected hot chilli/chile and can aid digestion. Even if there is nothing else in a modern Middle Eastern kitchen, there will be a pot of yogurt.

MAKING YOGURT WITH MILK

The standard ratio for yogurt to milk is 1 generous tablespoon live yogurt to 600 ml/2½ cups whole, or semi-skimmed/low-fat milk. For thicker yogurt, you can add 1-2 tablespoons of powdered milk to the milk that is boiling in the pan.

First, bring the milk to the boil in a large, heavy-based saucepan. When it starts to bubble, reduce the heat and leave it to simmer for 2–3 minutes. Turn off the heat and leave the milk to cool to a temperature that is bearable to dip your finger into. Beat the yogurt in a

deep bowl and strain a little of the milk into it, beating all the time. Strain the rest of the milk into the bowl and beat well. Cover the bowl with clingfilm/plastic wrap, or a clean tea/dish towel pulled tightly over it, and cover the whole bowl with a bath towel or blanket, tucking the edges around it to keep it warm. Place the wrapped bowl in a warm place for at least 6 hours, or overnight, to ferment and thicken a little. Unwrap the bowl and place it in the refrigerator for 2–3 hours, until it has set and is ready to use for numerous dishes.

Little yogurt balls with harissa and green olives

Draining yogurt until it resembles cream cheese is an ancient tradition in the eastern Mediterranean. Called 'labna' or 'labneh' in the region, this yogurt cheese is often used for mezze dips and fillings for poached fruit but it can also be taken one step further by draining it for longer until the yogurt cheese is firm enough to mould into delicate balls that can be stored in olive oil, 'labna bi zeit', and served as mezze with a sprinkling of herbs, paprika or with harissa. A great favourite on the mezze tables of Jordan, Syria and Lebanon, these yogurt cheese balls take 2–3 days to make to get the right consistency but they are well worth the effort and can be stored in a jar and kept for special occasions.

1 kg/4 ¼ cups thick creamy yogurt

1 teaspoon sea salt

2–3 tablespoons olive oil

2–3 teaspoons Harissa (page 14)

2–3 tablespoons stoned/pitted green olives, finely chopped

1 unwaxed lemon, cut into quarters, to serve

muslin/cheesecloth

sterilized jar (optional)

Serves 4–6

In a bowl combine the yogurt with the salt then tip it into a piece of muslin/cheesecloth suspended above a bowl or lining a colander set over a bowl (page 18). Fold the cloth over the yogurt and leave it to drain in a cool place – pour off the whey as it accumulates. Remove the drained yogurt from the cloth and leave it to dry out in a cool place for about 6 hours.

Lightly oil the finger and palms of your hands and roll small portions of the yogurt cheese into 2-cm/1-in. wide balls. Place the balls on a dish or tray, cover with clingfilm/plastic wrap and chill in the refrigerator for 6–12 hours.

Put the balls in a bowl and add the olive oil and harissa. Scatter the chopped olives over the top and serve with wedges of lemon to squeeze over them.

Alternatively, put the plain balls into a sterilized jar, pour in enough olive oil to cover them and keep them in a cool place for 2–3 weeks to serve as a snack when you want.

Fried halloumi with dried figs, black olives and zahtar

Salty and firm, halloumi is a fairly versatile cheese from the eastern Mediterranean. In Lebanon, Syria, and Cyprus (Turkish and Greek) it is made from cow's milk and matured in whey, sometimes combined with nigella seeds, mint, or thyme. Once grilled or fried, it can be added to salads or rice dishes, it can be used as a filling for savoury pastries, or it can be served on its own as a snack with spices, herbs, or dips. My favourite way to enjoy halloumi is to fry it in olive oil, sprinkle it with salt and zahtar, and serve it as a warm nibble with a drink — the key is to serve it straight from the pan, as it cools quickly and becomes solid and rubbery in texture. When I stayed with an Armenian family, this combination of halloumi with dried figs and olives was served for breakfast with glasses of hot apple tea but it also works well as a mezze dish.

3–4 tablespoons olive oil

250 g/8 oz. plain halloumi, well rinsed and cut into thin, bite-size slices

4–6 dried figs, cut into thin slices

2 tablespoons crinkled, fleshy black olives

1–2 tablespoons grape or date molasses

1–2 tablespoons zahtar

a sprinkling of sea salt

1 lime, cut into quarters, to serve

Serves 4

Heat the oil in a heavy-based saucepan. Add the halloumi and fry for 4–5 minutes until golden-brown all over. Drain on paper towels.

Tip the halloumi onto a serving dish, scatter the sliced figs and olives over and around it and drizzle the grape molasses over the top. Sprinkle with zahtar and a little salt to taste and serve immediately, while the halloumi is still warm, with wedges of lime to squeeze over it.

Brown beans with soft-boiled eggs and dukkah dressing

Like chickpeas and lentils, beans have been regarded as a staple of the poor. However, because the traditional dishes they are employed in are so delicious, the rich have never been able to resist them as described in the Egyptian proverb: 'The man of good breeding eats beans and returns to his breeding'. There are many popular varieties in the Middle East, including black-eyed, haricot and borlotti beans, all of which are used in fresh salads and tomato-based ragouts and soups. There are two types of broad (fava) bean – the common large, fresh green broad bean, 'ful akhdar', which is called 'ful nabed' when it is dried, and the small brown broad bean, 'ful baladi', also known as the Egyptian brown bean, which is dried before using and is dusty brown in colour. The most popular dish prepared with these Egyptian brown beans is a traditional peasant salad, 'ful medames', which is served as breakfast to the workers in the fields, or is tucked into pitta bread pockets at street stalls and eaten as a snack at any time of day. You can also find elaborate versions of it served as mezze in private homes and restaurants. Traditionally, the cooked beans are spooned into individual bowls and everyone helps themselves to dressings, condiments, chopped onions, eggs and herbs.

250 g/1½ cups Egyptian brown beans, soaked in plenty of water for 8 hours

3–4 eggs

2–3 tablespoons Dukkah (page 12)

2 tablespoons olive oil

freshly squeezed juice of 2 unwaxed lemons

2–3 garlic cloves, crushed

2 teaspoons honey

1–2 tablespoons orange blossom water

1 red onion, cut into bite-size pieces

a bunch of fresh flat-leaf parsley, roughly chopped

sea salt and freshly ground black pepper

a small bunch of fresh mint leaves, finely shredded

Serves 4–6

Drain the beans and put them into a deep saucepan. Fill the pan with water, bring it to the boil, reduce the heat and simmer for about 1 hour, until the beans are tender but still retain a bite to them.

Meanwhile, place the eggs in a pan of water, bring them to the boil for 4 minutes, then drain, refresh and peel them. Cut the eggs into quarters and put aside.

In a small bowl, mix together the dukkah spice mix with the olive oil, lemon juice and garlic. Stir in the honey and orange blossom water and season with salt and pepper.

Drain the beans, refresh them under cold water and tip them into a serving bowl. Scatter the onions and parsley over the beans and arrange the eggs on top. Pour the dressing over the salad, garnish with the mint and serve the beans with chunks of bread and other mezze dishes.

Smoked aubergine dip with tahini and parsley

Commonly known as 'baba ghanoush' ('baba ghannuj') in Lebanon, Syria, Jordan, Israel and the Palestinian Territories, this classic smoked aubergine/eggplant dip is also called 'moutabal'. Again, there are variations of this classic dish throughout the region as some cooks add chopped flat-leaf parsley or coriander/cilantro while others lighten it with a little yogurt or lemon juice. There are also many similar mezze dishes prepared with smoked aubergine/eggplant without the tahini. In essence, baba ghanoush should be creamy with a strong smoky flavour. It is best enjoyed with warm crusty bread or strips of pitta bread, to dip into it.

2 large aubergines/eggplants

2–3 tablespoons tahini

freshly squeezed juice of 1–2 unwaxed lemons

2 garlic cloves, crushed

a small bunch of fresh flat-leaf parsley, roughly chopped

sea salt and freshly ground black pepper

olive oil, for drizzling

charcoal grill (optional)

Serves 4–6

Place the aubergines/eggplants directly over a gas flame or charcoal grill. Use tongs to turn them from time to time, until they have softened and the skin is charred and flaky. Place the aubergines/eggplants in a plastic bag for a minute to sweat and, when cool enough to handle, hold them by the stems under cold running water and peel off the skin. Squeeze out the excess water and place the flesh on a chopping board. (If using a charcoal grill, the skin toughens instead of charring, so it is easier to slit the aubergine/eggplant open like a canoe and scoop out the softened flesh). Chop the flesh to a pulp.

In a bowl, beat the aubergine/eggplant pulp with the tahini and lemon juice to a creamy paste. Add the garlic and most of the parsley and season well with salt and pepper. Beat the mixture thoroughly and tip it into a serving bowl. Drizzle a little olive oil over the top to keep it moist and garnish with a sprinkle of chopped parsley.

Roasted red pepper and walnut dip

This wonderful, medieval Arab dip, 'muhammara', can be found in southern Turkey, Lebanon, Syria, Jordan, Iraq and parts of North and East Africa. It's delicious served as a mezze dish with strips of toasted Arab flatbreads or crudités, or as a sauce for grilled fish, chicken or 'kibbeh'.

3 red (bell) peppers

2 fresh red chillies/chiles

4–6 garlic cloves

150 ml/⅔ cup olive oil

150 g/1 generous cup shelled walnuts

3 generous tablespoons white breadcrumbs

2 tablespoons pomegranate syrup/molasses or freshly squeezed juice of 1 lemon, plus some for garnishing

2 teaspoons honey

1–2 teaspoons ground cumin

a small bunch of fresh flat-leaf parsley, finely chopped

sea salt

toasted flatbread, to serve

ovenproof dish

baking sheet

Serves 4–6

Preheat the oven to 200°C (400°F) Gas 6.

Put the red (bell) peppers into an ovenproof dish with the chillies/chiles and garlic, drizzle with half the olive oil and put them in the preheated oven to roast for about 1 hour. Turn the (bell) peppers and chillies/chiles from time to time in the oil until the skins are slightly burnt and buckled. Remove the chillies/chiles and garlic at this point but leave the peppers for the full hour or longer.

Put the walnuts on a baking sheet; place them in the oven for the last 10 minutes of the cooking time, so that they are lightly toasted and emitting a lovely nutty aroma.

Peel the skins off the peppers, chillies/chiles and garlic and remove any seeds. Roughly chop the flesh and put it into a food processer with the walnuts, breadcrumbs, pomegranate syrup/molasses or lemon juice, honey and cumin. Pour in the roasting oil and whiz to a purée. Drizzle in the rest of the oil whilst whizzing, add most of the parsley and season well with salt.

Tip the mixture into a serving bowl, swirl a little pomegranate syrup/molasses or lemon juice over the top and sprinkle with the rest of the parsley. Serve with toasted flatbread.

Hot hummus with samna and pine nuts

This heavenly hummus is a gem of a dish from eastern Anatolia. I first had it baked in a clay dish in a tiny village near Kars 25 years ago and I have been writing about it and enthusiastically devouring it ever since. The word 'hummus' means 'chickpea' in Arabic but also refers to the ubiquitous dip made with chickpeas and olive oil, versions of which you can find all over the Middle East but, to my mind, this recipe is simply the most delicious way to enjoy it. The traditional Anatolian dish, 'sicak humus', is thicker and heavier than the one I make as I add yogurt to it to make it lighter, more mousse-like and utterly moreish!

2 x 400-g/14.5 oz. cans of chickpeas, drained and rinsed

2 teaspoons cumin seeds

2–3 garlic cloves, crushed

roughly 4 tablespoons olive oil

freshly squeezed juice of 2 unwaxed lemons

2 tablespoons tahini

6 tablespoons thick, creamy yogurt

sea salt and freshly ground black pepper

2–3 tablespoons pine nuts

2 tablespoons Samna (page 13) or butter

crusty bread or toasted pitta bread, and marinated olives, to serve

Serves 4–6

Preheat the oven to 200°C (400°F) Gas 6.

Instead of using a pestle and mortar to pound the chickpeas to a paste in the traditional manner, make life easy and tip the chickpeas into an electric blender or a food processor. Add the cumin seeds, garlic, olive oil and lemon and whiz the mixture to a thick paste. Add the tahini and continue to whiz until the mixture is really thick and smooth. Add the yogurt and whiz until the mixture has loosened a little and the texture is creamy. Season to taste with salt and pepper and tip the mixture into an ovenproof dish.

Dry-roast the pine nuts in a small pan until they begin to brown and emit a nutty aroma. Then add the samna or butter to the pine nuts in the pan and stir until it melts. Pour the melted samna or butter over the hummus, spoon the pine nuts all over the surface and pop the dish into the preheated oven for about 25 minutes, until the hummus has risen a little and most of the samna or butter has been absorbed.

Serve immediately – the hummus is best when it is still hot – with chunks of warm crusty bread or strips of toasted pitta bread and marinated olives.

Spicy broad bean balls with yogurt and tahini

Regarded as their national dish by several countries and communities, such as Egypt, Jordan, Israel and the Palestinian Territories – falafel are popular wherever you go in the Middle East. Certainly the Christian Copts of Egypt, who are believed to be true representatives of the ancient Egyptians, have traditionally prepared falafel (they call them 'ta'amia') for their religious festivals, particularly during Lent when they are not allowed to eat meat. Any-time-of-day street food, great takeaway food and a tasty mezze dish, falafel can be prepared with dried chickpeas or dried broad/fava beans, or a combination of the two. Tuck a couple of freshly fried falafel into the hollow pocket of a toasted pitta bread with a sprinkling of sliced red onion, roughly chopped flat-leaf parsley and pickles of your choice; add a little chilli paste, such as Harissa (page 14) or Zhug (page 15), a drizzle of tahini and a dollop of yogurt, and you have the most deliciously healthy Middle Eastern equivalent to a fast-food burger!

Drain the broad/fava beans, put them into a food processor and blend to a smooth soft paste – this can take quite a long time. Add 4 of the crushed garlic cloves, salt, cumin, coriander, chilli powder and baking powder and continue to blend the paste. Add most of the parsley, the coriander/cilantro and spring onions/scallions and blend the mixture briefly. Leave the mixture to rest for 1–2 hours.

Meanwhile, beat the yogurt in a bowl with the remaining garlic cloves. Season well to taste and put aside.

Mould the broad/fava bean mixture into small, tight balls and place them on a plate. Heat up enough oil for deep-frying in a pan and fry the broad/fava bean balls in batches, until golden brown. Drain them on paper towels.

Tip the falafel onto a serving dish and garnish with the reserved coriander/cilantro. Serve them with the yogurt mixture, sprinkled with sumac, along with harissa, toasted pitta bread, chopped red onion and chilli/chile peppers.

350 g/2 cups large, skinless, dried broad/fava beans, soaked in cold water for 24 hours

6 garlic cloves, crushed

1–2 teaspoons sea salt

2 teaspoons ground cumin

2 teaspoons ground coriander

1 scant teaspoon chilli powder

1 teaspoon baking powder

a bunch of fresh flat-leaf parsley, finely chopped

a bunch of fresh coriander/cilantro, finely chopped, plus some for garnishing

4 spring onions/scallions, finely chopped

400 g/1⅔ cups thick, creamy yogurt

sea salt and freshly ground black pepper

sunflower oil, for frying

1 teaspoon sumac; Harissa (page 14); toasted pitta bread; 1 small red onion, roughly chopped; and a handful of small green chilli/chile peppers, to serve

Serves 4–6

Yogurt with cucumber, walnuts and sultanas

In Turkey, Iran and the eastern Mediterranean, there are many yogurt-based mezze dishes, which can be classed as salads or dips, depending on how you serve them. Cucumber, garlic and mint are classic combinations with yogurt, such as the well-known tzatziki in neighbouring Greece, of which there are several variations in Lebanon, Syria and Turkey. In Iran, there is this unusual, textured yogurt and cucumber salad, 'mast o-khiyar', which can be served as a dip with bread, and adds a touch of elegance to the table when it is decorated with fresh rose petals.

1 large cucumber

sea salt

2 tablespoons sultanas/golden raisins

2 tablespoons rose water

700 g/3 cups thick, creamy yogurt

2 cloves garlic, crushed

4–6 fresh chives, finely chopped or snipped with scissors

2 tablespoons toasted walnuts, coarsely chopped

a small bunch of fresh mint, finely chopped

1 teaspoon dried mint

1 sweet-scented pink, yellow, or red rose head, to serve

Serves 4

Peel the cucumber in strips, leaving some of the skin on, cut it in quarters lengthways and slice it finely. Sprinkle the slices with salt and leave them to weep for 5-10 minutes.

Put the sultanas/golden raisins into a small bowl with the rose water and leave them to soak for 10 minutes.

Beat the yogurt in bowl with the garlic. Stir in the chives and walnuts. Using your hands, squeeze the cucumber slices over a bowl to press out the excess water and add them to the yogurt. Drain the sultanas/golden raisins, discard the rose water, and add them to the yogurt with the mint.

Season the salad with salt and spoon it into a serving bowl. Sprinkle the dried mint over the top and garnish it with rose petals. Serve as a salad with other mezze dishes, or as dip on its own with chunks of warm, fresh, crusty bread.

Orange salad with dates, chillies and preserved lemon

This attractive and refreshing salad is a delicious addition to any mezze spread, or it can be served as an accompaniment to spicy meat or poultry dishes. There are different versions of this salad throughout the Middle East. Some include slices of fresh lemon or lime, while others add onions and black olives instead of dates and preserved lemon, but all are sweet, juicy and slightly salty. This recipe is Moroccan but you find oranges combined with dates in Iraq, Jordan and Egypt.

4 ripe, sweet oranges

175 g/1 cup moist dried dates, stoned/pitted

1 fresh red chilli/chile, seeded and finely sliced

the peel of 1 preserved lemon (page 17), finely sliced

2–3 tablespoons orange blossom water

a small bunch of fresh coriander/cilantro, roughly chopped

Serves 4–6

Peel the oranges, removing as much of the pith as possible. Place the oranges on a plate to catch the juice and finely slice them into circles, removing any pips. Tip the oranges into a bowl with the juice, or arrange them in a shallow dish.

Finely slice the dates, lengthways, and scatter them over the oranges. Scatter the sliced chilli/chile and preserved lemon over the top and splash the orange blossom water over the salad. Leave the flavours to mingle for at least 10 minutes, garnish with the coriander/cilantro and toss very gently just before serving.

Little spinach and feta pastries with pine nuts

The variety of savoury and sweet pastries in the Middle East is endless, particularly in the eastern Mediterranean region and Morocco. The savoury ones are generally prepared with puff and flaky pastry doughs or with a traditional paper-thin flat bread called 'yufka' in Turkey and 'ouarka' in Morocco but mainly known as 'fila' throughout the rest of the region. The pastries vary from layered or stuffed pies served as a main course to little individual pastries, which can be served as mezze or as little snacks. Stuffed with ingredients like spinach, pumpkin, dry-cured beef, shellfish and cheese, these little pastries are known as 'fatayer' or 'sambusak' in the Levant, 'börek' in Turkey, and 'brik' in Morocco and Tunisia. They come in a variety of shapes and sizes, ranging from half moons, tiny kayaks and rolled cigars to square packages and triangles.

500 g/1 lb. fresh spinach leaves, trimmed, washed and drained

2 tablespoons olive oil

1 tablespoon butter

2 onions, chopped

3 generous tablespoons pine nuts

freshly squeezed juice of 1 unwaxed lemon

1 teaspoon ground allspice

150 g/5 oz. feta cheese, crumbled

a small bunch of fresh dill, finely chopped

sea salt and freshly ground black pepper

plain/all-purpose flour, for dusting

450 g/16 oz. ready-prepared puff pastry, thawed if frozen

extra olive oil, for brushing

10-cm/4-in. round pastry cutter

2 baking sheets lined with aluminium foil

Serves 6

Preheat the oven to 180°C (350°F) Gas 4.

Steam the spinach until it has softened, then drain and refresh under running cold water before squeezing out the excess liquid with your hands. Place the spinach on a wooden board and chop it coarsely.

Heat the oil and butter in a heavy-based pan and stir in the onion to soften. Add 2 tablespoons of the pine nuts and cook for 2–3 minutes until both the onions and pine nuts begin to turn golden. Stir in the spinach with the lemon juice and allspice and lightly fold in the crumbled feta and dill. Season the mixture with salt and pepper and leave to cool.

Lightly dust a surface with flour and roll the pastry into a thin sheet. Using a pastry cutter or the rim of a cup, cut out as many 10 cm/4 in. rounds as you can and pile them up, lightly dusting them with flour. Take each round and spoon a little of the spinach mixture in the middle. Pull up the sides to make a pyramid by pinching the edges with your fingertips. It does not matter if one of the sides opens during cooking to reveal the filling; that is part of their appeal.

Line the baking sheets with aluminium foil and place the pastries on them. Brush the tops with a little oil and bake them in the preheated oven for about 30 minutes, until golden brown.

Roughly 5 minutes before taking the pastries out of the oven, spread the remaining tablespoon of pine nuts onto a small piece of aluminium foil and toast them in the oven until they turn golden brown. Once you have placed the little pastries on a plate, sprinkle the toasted pine nuts over them and serve while they are still hot.

Parsley salad with bulgur and pomegranate seeds

Throughout the Middle East, there are numerous variations of this traditional Lebanese and Syrian salad, tabbouleh – some prepared with tomatoes and onions, others with chickpeas, mint and oregano and, in Turkey, there is a delicious version called 'kisir', which is prepared with tomato paste, chillies/chiles and masses of mint and parsley. Traditionally, though, tabbouleh is primarily a parsley salad, flavoured with a hint of mint and tossed with a small quantity of fine bulgur so that the grains resemble tiny gems in a sea of green. Fine-grain bulgur is available in Middle Eastern stores and some supermarkets. The key to the preparation of this salad is to slice the parsley finely, rather than chop it, so that the fine strands remain dry and fresh, not mushy, and to dress it at the last minute.

60 g/½ cup fine bulgur

freshly squeezed juice of 2 unwaxed lemons

a large bunch of fresh flat-leaf parsley

a bunch of fresh mint leaves

4 spring onions/scallions, trimmed and finely sliced

seeds of 1 pomegranate

1–2 tablespoons olive oil

2 tablespoons pomegranate syrup/molasses

sea salt and freshly ground black pepper

1 head of cos/romaine lettuce leaves

Serves 4–6

Rinse the bulgur in cold water and drain well. Place it in a bowl and pour over the lemon juice – if you need to, add a little warm water so that there is enough liquid to just cover the bulgur. Leave it to soften for 10 minutes while you prepare the rest of the salad.

Place the parsley on a chopping board and hold the bunch tightly with one hand while you slice the leaves and the tops of the stalks as finely as you can with a sharp knife. Tip the sliced parsley into a bowl. Slice the mint leaves in the same way and add them to the bowl. Add the spring onions/scallions, most of the pomegranate seeds and the soaked bulgur.

Gently stir in the oil and pomegranate syrup/molasses. Season the salad with salt and pepper to taste and garnish with the reserved pomegranate seeds. Serve immediately, so that the herbs do not get the chance to soften, with the lettuce leaves arranged around the salad to be used as a scoop for the tabbouleh.

Bread: a gift from God

Throughout the Middle East, bread is regarded as a gift from God. It is treated with respect and never thrown away; instead it is employed in a multitude of dishes. Traditionally, it is broken by the hand as to cut it with a knife would be tantamount to lifting a sword against God's blessing and, if a bit of bread falls to the ground, it is picked up and held to the lips and forehead as a gesture of atonement.

It is thought that the first cereal crops were grown in Syria, Persia, and Anatolia before 7000 BC and there are records of skilled bakers amongst the ancient Egyptians, Phoenicians and the Cappadocians. Tribal communities would have cooked bread dough on flat stones placed in the embers of a fire, or a metal sheet placed over the flames. This would have gradually developed into the creation of an outdoor clay oven in which both unleavened and leavened breads could be baked. The first leavened breads are attributed to the ancient Egytpians and the Israelites left their leaven behind when they fled in the Exodus from Egypt and had to exist on unleavened bread.

In medieval times, wheat was the primary cereal employed in bread making, although the poorer communities used barley and millet, and the dough was often flavoured with spices or filled with sweet and scented concoctions of dried fruit, nuts, tahini or honey. An outdoor oven ('tandoor' in Arabic) was used for unleavened doughs. Large communal ovens ('furn') could accommodate leavened doughs in the bottom, whilst the unleavened ones were stretched out and stuck to the sides. More sophisticated unleavened and leavened breads emerged during the Ottoman period. Thin flat breads were rolled into wide, paper-thin rounds and experimented with in layered dishes involving savoury and sweet fillings, such as the ubiquitous baklava.

Today in the Middle East, bread making is taken for granted as it is a part of daily life wherever you go.

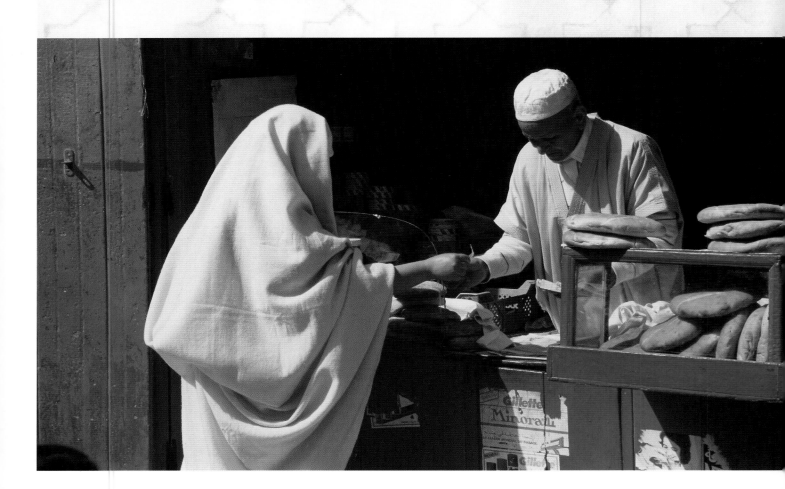

Almost every village has a baker who produces batches of fresh bread ('khubz' in Arabic and 'ekmek' in Turkish) two or three times a day, or there is a communal oven to bake doughs that have been prepared at home. Most locals would be lost without their daily loaf — it is a regional staple and in some communities it replaces cutlery. The day often begins with fresh bread and honey or jam, tahini, combined with a fruit molasses, pulse dishes, cheese and olives and, at every meal, it serves as a scoop for mezze dishes and dips, a mop for all the delicious garlicky and spicy sauces, and as a palate cleanser in-between courses.

The most common bread in the Middle East is the flat bread with a hollow pouch ('khubz' or 'eish shami'), known as pitta bread outside the region, but there are many versions of it. There are many other regional flat breads, each with their own characteristic, such as an Egyptian whole-wheat version ('eish baladi'), the Iranian loaves ('nan'), and a variety of Turkish pide. Some of these regional breads contain hollow pouches, while others may include yogurt in the dough resulting in a thicker and spongier texture. The round rings of bread dough ('semit') sprinkled with sesame or nigella seeds are also very common. Paper-thin sheets ('fila'), made from bread dough but used like a pastry (as they are brushed with butter and layered in savoury and sweet dishes) are ubiquitous, from Iran to Morocco. Jews often prepare leavened bread using eggs in the dough and their festive breads can be sweet and aromatic. In Turkey and Morocco, there are leavened village breads made with corn, while the the daily bread of Turkey and Iran is a golden-crusted, leavened loaf, shaped like a kayak with the texture of a baguette.

Stale or leftover bread always has a delicious destination, particularly in the peasant dishes of Lebanon, Syria and Jordan. Many village soups are thickened with bread and there is of course the popular toasted bread salad, fattoush. There are also many sweet dishes prepared with leftover bread, often soaked in a fruit syrup or honey and served with poached fruit spooned over the top. Perhaps the most popular of all are the numerous 'fatta' dishes comprising stale or toasted bread that has been soaked in stock and piled high with vegetables, pulses, or meat and topped with a generous dollop of yogurt. The Prophet Mohammad is said to have been so partial to this dish, which was known as 'tharid' at that time in Arabia, that he praised his favourite wife by comparing her to it: 'A'isha surpasses other women as tharid surpasses other dishes.'

There is undoubtedly a certain mystique surrounding the preparation and enjoyment of bread in the Middle East, and it has been written about in poetry and in cookery manuals since medieval times. It plays an important role in different religious practices and festivities, some displaying stronger superstitious feelings than others. Orthodox Jews break bread and bless it at every meal; Muslims break the fast during Ramadan with bread; Christians bake special breads for Easter; and some bakers bless the dough as they knead it. But nothing quite puts the superstition into perspective as the sight of a starving man kissing a morsel of bread before eating it.

Bread and parsley salad with pomegranate syrup and sumac

2 pitta breads or 3 slices of crusty bread, toasted and broken into bite-size pieces

3 tablespoons olive oil

freshly squeezed juice of 1 unwaxed lemon

½ cos/romaine lettuce, trimmed and chopped

2–3 tomatoes, skinned, seeded and chopped

1 red or green (bell) pepper, seeded and chopped

1 red onion, halved lengthways and halved again crossways, finely sliced

a large bunch of fresh flat-leaf parsley, roughly chopped

2–3 tablespoons pomegranate syrup/molasses

2 teaspoons ground sumac

sea salt and freshly ground black pepper

Serves 4

Fresh, crunchy salads prepared with a combination of tomatoes, (bell) peppers, cucumber, onions and parsley vary throughout the region and are always popular with mezze or grilled meats but, in Syria and Lebanon, the addition of toasted bread transforms what is daily, peasant fare into the classic salad called 'fattoush'. Bread is regarded as a gift from Allah in the Muslim world; it is never wasted or thrown away so this is a good way of using up day-old bread, by toasting it and soaking it in olive oil before tossing it through the salad.

Put all the broken pieces of bread into a bowl and toss in 1 tablespoon of the olive oil and the lemon juice.

Place all the vegetables in another bowl and add the parsley and bread. Drizzle the rest of the olive oil and the pomegranate syrup/molasses over the salad and sprinkle with the sumac. Season with salt and pepper then leave the salad to sit for 15 minutes before tossing.

Serve as part of a mezze spread, or as an accompaniment to grilled and roasted meat, poultry and fish.

meat and poultry

Lamb and apricot tagine with ras el hanout

When it comes to combining fruit with meat and poultry in stews and tagines, the link between the culinary traditions of ancient Persia and Morocco becomes evident. As the Arab Islamic invasion spread to the far western shores of North Africa in the 7th century, it is very likely that some of the dishes they had acquired from ancient Persia would have travelled with them. This culinary invasion would have been repeated in the Golden Age of Islam when Baghdad was the centre of the culinary world and many dishes were based on the lavish traditions of the sophisticated Persian court cuisine. The same fruits are used in Morocco and the Middle East today, lending an air of medieval exoticness to the dishes – duck with quinces, beef with prunes, meatballs with cherries, chicken with grapes and lamb with apricots. Called 'mishmishiya' in most of the Middle East after the Arabic word for apricot, 'mishmish', this recipe is for a Moroccan version cooked in a traditional Berber tagine.

16 dried apricots, soaked in water for at least 2 hours

1–2 tablespoons Samna (page 13), or 1–2 tablespoons olive oil with a knob/pat of butter

1 onion, finely chopped

2–3 garlic cloves, finely chopped

40 g/1½ oz. piece of fresh ginger, peeled and finely chopped

2 teaspoons coriander seeds

2–3 cinnamon sticks

2 teaspoons ras el hanout

700 g/1¾ lbs. lean lamb, trimmed and cut into bite-size pieces

1–2 tablespoons runny honey

1–2 tablespoons orange blossom water

sea salt and freshly ground black pepper

a small bunch of fresh coriander/cilantro, finely chopped

Serves 4

Drain the apricots and reserve the soaking water in a measuring jug/pitcher. Put half the apricots in a blender or a food processor with 2–3 tablespoons of the soaking water and blend to a purée. If necessary, top up the rest of the soaking liquid with water so that you have roughly 700 ml/3 cups.

Heat the samna, or olive oil and butter in the base of a tagine or in a heavy-based casserole dish and stir in the onion and garlic for 2–3 minutes. Add the fresh ginger, coriander seeds, cinnamon sticks and ras el hanout, then toss in the chunks of lamb, coating them in the onion and spices. Pour in the apricot soaking water with enough plain water to just cover the lamb. Bring the liquid to the boil, reduce the heat, put the lid on the tagine and simmer for about 30 minutes.

Add the whole apricots and continue to simmer for 15 minutes. Stir in the honey and the puréed apricots and simmer for a further 10–15 minutes. Splash in the orange blossom water, season with salt and pepper and scatter the coriander/cilantro over the top. Serve immediately with rice, bulgur, couscous or chunks of crusty loaf.

Meat loaf with saffron onions, sultanas and pine nuts

Both Syria and Lebanon claim 'kibbeh' ('kubba' in Iraq and 'kobeba' in Egypt), as their national dish but there are numerous versions throughout the Middle East. A pounded mixture of minced/ground meat and bulgur moulded into shapes and grilled, fried or baked, kibbeh cross all religious and national divides – they are a favourite festive food for Christians, Muslims, Jews, Kurds, Armenians and anyone else who wants cook vast quantities to share at ceremonial and family feasts. The culinary calendar of the Eastern Mediterranean tends to flow from one Islamic religious feast to another, interspersed with Christian feasts such as Christmas, Easter and St. Helena's Day, so street vendors do a steady trade in fried and grilled kibbeh all year round. One of my favourite kibbeh dishes is a homely baked one, 'kibbeh bil sanieh', which can be filled or topped with onions and served with a tomato sauce or tahini.

500 g/1 lb. 2 oz. finely minced/ground lean lamb, beef or veal

1 onion, grated

2 teaspoons ground cinnamon

1 teaspoon baharat mix

1 teaspoon ground allspice

sea salt and freshly ground black pepper

350 g/2⅓ cups fine or medium grain bulgur, rinsed and drained

2 tablespoons Samna (page 13), or 2 tablespoons olive oil with a knob/pat of butter

shallow oven-proof dish/tin (10 cm/4 in. in diameter, if using a round one), greased

FOR THE TOPPING

2–3 tablespoons olive oil

2–3 onions, halved and sliced with the grain

2 tablespoons pine nuts

2 tablespoons sultanas/golden raisins

a pinch of saffron fronds/threads, soaked in 2 tablespoons warm water

sea salt and freshly ground black pepper

1–2 tablespoons pomegranate syrup/molasses (optional)

Serves 4–6

Preheat the oven to 180°C (350°F) Gas 4.

In a bowl pound the minced/ground meat with the onion and spices. Season with plenty of salt and pepper and knead well. Add the bulgur and knead for about 10 minutes, until the mixture is thoroughly mixed and pasty. Alternatively, you can place the mixture in a blender or a food processor and blend to a paste.

Tip the mixture into the greased dish and spread it evenly. Flatten the top with your knuckles and spread the samna, or olive oil and butter over the surface. Using a sharp knife, cut the mixture into wedges or diamond shapes and pop it into the preheated oven for about 30 minutes, until nicely browned.

Meanwhile, prepare the topping by heating the oil in a frying pan/skillet and stir in the onions, until they begin to brown. Add the pine nuts and sultanas/raisins for 2 minutes, then stir in the saffron water. Season with salt and pepper.

When the kibbeh is ready, spread the onion mixture over the top and return it to the oven for 5 minutes. Cut it into portions and arrange them on a serving dish before drizzling a little pomegranate syrup/molasses over the top, if desired.

Roast lamb stuffed with bulgur, apricots, dates and nuts

FOR THE STUFFING

225 g/1½ cups medium grain or coarse bulgur

2 tablespoons Samna (page 13), or 2 tablespoons olive oil with a knob/pat of butter

1 onion, finely chopped

2 teaspoons cumin seeds

2 teaspoons coriander seeds

1–2 teaspoons granulated sugar

2 teaspoons ground turmeric

1–2 teaspoons ground cinnamon

1–2 teaspoons ground allspice

125 g/4 oz. minced/ground beef

120 g/1 scant cup pine nuts

120 g/1 scant cup unsalted pistachios, chopped

a bunch of fresh coriander/cilantro, finely chopped

a bunch of fresh flat-leaf parsley, finely chopped

sea salt and freshly ground black pepper

FOR THE LAMB

1 large (bone-in) breast of lamb, with a pouch cut between the skin and the ribs, rinsed and patted dry

1–2 tablespoons melted Samna (page 13) or 1–2 tablespoons olive oil, for rubbing

225 g/1½ cups dried apricots, soaked overnight in just enough cold water to cover

2–3 tablespoons granulated sugar

2 tablespoons orange blossom water

Serves 4–6

For ceremonial and religious feasts, such as the Muslim Eid el Kurban, which marks the near-sacrifice of Isma'il, (Isaac in the Bible), it is traditional to slaughter a ram and spit roast it over a pit dug in the earth. Roasting whole beasts in this manner can vary throughout the region, such as the Bedouin's festive dish, 'mansaf', meaning 'big dish'. Traditionally this consists of a huge flat tray lined with sheets of flatbread covered with a layer of rice, on top of which the whole spit-roasted lamb, kid or even a baby camel, sits. In Jordan, mansaf has become the national dish and is prepared in gigantic proportions for weddings and state banquets where you can find a baby camel stuffed with a sheep which is in turn stuffed with a turkey, just like a Russian doll. In Saudi Arabia, the national dish for festive occasions is either 'qouzi mahshi', roasted stuffed kid, or 'kharouf mahshi', roasted milk-fed lamb, both of which are served with a mountain of rice and hard-boiled eggs. Another Middle Eastern ceremonial dish is the Persian-inspired 'dala' mahshi', a breast of lamb stuffed with minced/ground beef, rice or bulgur, and dried fruit. This is easier to prepare at home and the stuffing can vary according to your taste. It is also worth asking your butcher to prepare the breast for you by cutting a pouch for the stuffing between the skin and the ribs.

Preheat the oven to 200°C (400°F) Gas 6.

First prepare the stuffing. Rinse the bulgur and tip it into a bowl. Cover with just enough boiling water and leave it to swell for 10 minutes.

Melt the samna, or olive oil and butter in a heavy-based pan and stir in the onion, cumin seeds, coriander seeds and sugar for 2–3 minutes, until the onion begins to colour. Stir in the turmeric, cinnamon and allspice then add the minced/ground lamb and cook until it begins to brown. Toss in the bulgur, nuts, coriander/cilantro and parsley, season to taste and leave the mixture to cool in the pan.

When cool, stuff the breast pouch of the lamb with the bulgur filling – if there is any left over it can be served with the meat afterwards. Rub the joints with a little samna or olive oil and then place the breast in the preheated oven for about 1 hour, until the meat is well browned and tender.

Meanwhile, prepare the apricots. Drain the apricots and tip the soaking water into a heavy-based pan. Add the sugar and bring the liquid to the boil, stirring until the sugar dissolves. Boil gently for 2 minutes, then stir in the orange blossom water and the apricots. Bring the liquid back to the boil, reduce the heat and simmer for 10–15 minutes.

Take the lamb breast out of the oven and spoon off any excess fat from the roasting dish. Baste the meat with the juices, spoon the apricots over the top and return the dish to the oven for 10 minutes, until nicely glazed and slightly caramelized. Serve immediately with a salad.

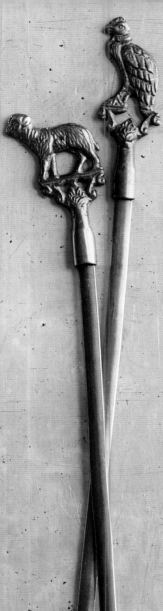

Lamb shish kebab with yogurt and flat bread

When people think of Middle Eastern food, kebabs/kabobs often spring to mind – in particular the ubiquitous Turkish 'döner' kebab/kabob ('shawarma' in Arabic), which traditionally consists of thin slices of tender, marinated lamb threaded onto a vertical spit, interpersed with pieces of fat and onion, which is roasted as the spit rotates in front of a fire and the meat is expertly sliced off as it cooks. Another well-known kebab/kabob is the Turkish 'sis kebab', meaning that it is cooked on a sword; it was said to have come into existence when the Ottoman troops camped out and cooked their meat on the end of their swords over an open fire. Called 'shashlik' or 'lahma mashwi' in Arabic, there are variations of the traditional shish kebab/kabob throughout the Middle East but, to my mind, the Turkish version is the ultimate. Designed to use up day-old pide (Turkish bread), which can be substituted with pitta bread, the dish is succulent and tasty and should be devoured on its own. For this recipe, you need flat, broad metal skewers, which look like mini swords, as the mixture will not hold together well on thin, rounded skewers.

FOR THE KEBABS/KABOBS

500 g/1 lb. 2oz. lean minced/ground lamb

2 onions, finely chopped

1 fresh green chillies/chiles, seeded and finely chopped

4 garlic cloves, crushed

1 teaspoon finely chopped dried red chilli/chiles or paprika

1 teaspoon ground sumac

a bunch of fresh flat-leaf parsley, finely chopped

sea salt and freshly ground black pepper

8 fresh plum tomatoes

FOR THE SAUCE

2 tablespoons Samna (page 13), or

2 tablespoons olive oil with a knob/pat of butter

1 onion, finely chopped

2 garlic cloves, finely chopped

1 fresh green chilli/chile, seeded and finely chopped

1–2 teaspoons granulated sugar

a 400-g/14.5-oz. can of chopped tomatoes

sea salt and freshly ground black pepper

TO SERVE

4 pitta breads, cut into bite-size pieces

2 tablespoons butter

1 teaspoon ground sumac

1 teaspoon dried oregano

sea salt

a bunch of fresh flat-leaf parsley, roughly chopped

400 g/1⅔ cups thick, creamy yogurt

charcoal grill

6 broad metal skewers

Serves 4

Put the minced/ground lamb into a bowl. Add all the other kebab/kabob ingredients and knead well, until it resembles a smooth paste and is quite sticky. Cover and place in the refrigerator for about 15 minutes.

Meanwhile, make the sauce. Heat the samna, or olive oil and butter in a heavy-based pan. Stir in the onion, garlic and chilli/chile, and cook until they begin to colour. Add the sugar and tomatoes and cook, uncovered, until quite thick and saucy. Season to taste with salt and pepper. Keep warm.

Wet your hands to make the mixture easier to handle. Mould portions of the meat mixture around the skewers, squeezing and flattening it, so it looks like the sheath to the sword.

Prepare a charcoal grill. Thread the tomatoes onto skewers and place them and the meat skewers over the charcoal. While they are cooking, quickly prepare the pitta breads. Melt the butter in a heavy-based pan, add the pitta bread pieces and heat until golden. Sprinkle them with some of the sumac and oregano and arrange them on a serving dish, bearing in mind that they are the base for the whole dish. Splash a little sauce over the pitta breads.

As soon as the tomatoes are nicely charred, arrange them around the dish. When the kebabs/kabobs are cooked on both sides, slip the meat sheath off the skewer, cut it into bite-size pieces and arrange the pieces alternately with the tomatoes around the dish. Sprinkle salt over the top, along with the rest of the sumac and oregano. Garnish with parsley and serve hot with extra dollops of sauce and yogurt.

Aubergines stuffed with lamb and pine nuts

The Arabs fell under the spell of the aubergine/eggplant when they conquered Persia, although today in the Middle East, they are now often referred to as 'poor man's meat'. In Turkey, however, the aubergine/eggplant is regarded as the king of vegetables and there are over 200 dishes prepared with them, such as this Ottoman classic called 'karnıyarık' in Turkish, meaning 'split belly', which falls into the supreme category of 'etli dolma', consisting of cooked vegetables or leaves stuffed with aromatic meat fillings.

Preheat the oven to 200°C (400°F) Gas 6.

First prepare the filling. Put the lamb into a bowl with the onion and spices and knead well. Add the tomatoes, tomato purée/paste, 2 teaspoons sugar, pine nuts, currants, herbs and seasoning and knead for about 5 minutes, until thoroughly combined. Lift the mixture into the air and slap it down into the bowl to knock out the air. Repeat several times then cover the bowl and put aside for 30 minutes.

Meanwhile, using a sharp knife or a potato peeler, partially peel the aubergines/eggplants to leave thick stripes, like the markings of a zebra. Immerse the whole aubergines/eggplants in a bowl of salted water for 15 minutes then drain and pat dry with paper towels. Heat enough sunflower oil for frying in a heavy-based frying pan/skillet and pop in the aubergines/eggplants, two at time, rolling them in the oil until they are lightly browned all over and softened. Lift them out of the oil and drain on paper towels.

Using a knife or tongs, slit each aubergine/eggplant lengthways down the middle, taking care not to cut through the base and making sure you leave the ends intact, so that it resembles a kayak. Prise each slit open and divide the meat mixture among them, making sure the filling is tightly packed. Place a slice of tomato over the the meat filling at the head of the aubergine/eggplant and a strip of (bell) pepper lengthways below it, so that the tomato looks like a flower with a pepper stalk.

Place the stuffed aubergines/eggplants, side by side, in a baking dish. Mix together the olive oil, lemon juice, water and sugar and pour it over and around the aubergines/eggplants. Sprinkle a little salt over the top, cover the dish with aluminium foil and bake in the preheated oven for about 25 minutes. Remove the foil, dot the tops of the stuffed aubergines/eggplants with the butter, and return the dish to the oven for a further 25–30 minutes, until the meat is cooked and the aubergines/eggplants are tender.

Garnish the stuffed aubergines/eggplants with parsley and serve them hot with wedges of lemon to squeeze over them. Or, leave the aubergines/eggplants to cool in the dish and serve them at room temperature, moistened with a little of the cooking liquid.

FOR THE FILLING

175 g/16 oz. finely minced/ground lean lamb

1 onion, finely chopped

2 teaspoons ground cinnamon

1 teaspoon ground allspice

1 teaspoon ground cumin

2 large tomatoes, peeled, seeded and chopped

1 tablespoon tomato purée/paste

3 teaspoons granulated sugar

2 tablespoons pine nuts

2 tablespoons currants, soaked in water for 20 minutes and drained

a small bunch of fresh dill, finely chopped

a small bunch of fresh flat-leaf parsley, finely chopped

sea salt and freshly ground black pepper

4 medium aubergines/eggplants

sunflower oil, for frying

1 tomato, sliced into rounds

half a green (bell) pepper, stalk removed, seeded and cut into 4 thin strips

150 ml/⅔ cup olive oil

freshly squeezed juice of 1 unwaxed lemon

3 tablespoons water

1 teaspoon granulated sugar

sea salt

1 teaspoon butter

a small bunch of fresh flat-leaf parsely, finely chopped

1 unwaxed lemon, cut into wedges, to serve

Serves 4

Meatballs in an egg and lemon sauce

Meatballs, in the form of 'kofta' (kefta) or 'kibbeh', are perhaps the best known of all Middle Eastern meat dishes after the ubiquitous kebabs/kabobs. Infinite in variety, meatballs are part of an ancient Arab heritage and have remained as versatile food in street stalls, cafés, restaurants and in the home. Traditionally prepared with minced/ground beef, veal or lamb, the meat is pounded to a smooth texture with onions, spices and herbs, as well as ingredients such as nuts, dried fruits, breadcrumbs, rice and bulgur. They are then usually fried or grilled. There are several notable exceptions though, such as this Turkish dish, 'terbiyeli ekşili köfte', literally translated as 'well-behaved sour meatballs' as they are cooked in a sauce which is bound with a liaison of egg and lemon. Another legacy of the Ottoman Empire, created by the industrious chefs of the Palace kitchens, these particular meatballs travelled to the Balkans, Greece and parts of the eastern Mediterranean where they are popular amongst the Jewish communities.

FOR THE MEATBALLS

450 g/1 lb. finely minced/ground lean lamb

1 tablespoon medium or long-grain rice, washed and drained

a small bunch of fresh dill, finely chopped

a small bunch of fresh flat-leaf parsley, finely chopped

1–2 teaspoons sea salt

freshly ground black pepper

1–2 tablespoons plain/all-purpose flour

FOR THE SAUCE

1 litre/1 quart water

2 carrots, peeled and diced

1 small celeriac/celery root, peeled, trimmed and diced (kept in water with a squeeze of lemon juice to prevent it discolouring)

2 potatoes, peeled and diced

2 egg yolks

freshly squeezed juice of 2 unwaxed lemons

1 tablespoon Labna (page 18), prepared overnight, or plain, thick yogurt

1 teaspoon dried mint

a small bunch of fresh dill fronds, finely chopped

Put the lamb into a bowl with the rice, dill, parsley, salt and a good grinding of black pepper. Knead the mixture together for about 5 minutes, until thoroughly combined, and slap the mixture down into the bottom of the bowl to knock out the air — this is important to prevent the meatballs from coming apart when cooking in the liquid.

Take small portions of the mixture into the palm of your hand and mould them into tight, cherry-size balls. Spoon the flour onto a flat surface and roll the balls in it until lightly coated. Put them aside.

Pour the water into a heavy-based, shallow saucepan and bring it to the boil. Drop in the carrots and celeriac/celery root, drained of the lemon water, and cook the vegetables for about 5 minutes. Keep the water boiling and drop in the meatballs. Reduce the heat, cover the saucepan and simmer for about 15 minutes. Add the potatoes and simmer, uncovered, for a further 15–20 minutes.

In a bowl, beat the egg yolks with the lemon juice, labna and mint. Spoon a little of the cooking liquid into the mixture then tip it all into the pan, stirring all the time, until it is heated through and the sauce has thickened. Be careful not to bring the liquid to the boil as it will curdle.

Serve the meatballs straight from the saucepan into shallow bowls and spoon the sauce around them. Garnish with the dill and serve with fresh bread or plain rice to mop up the sauce.

Serves 4–6

Roasted meat-stuffed onions with honey and tamarind

Stuffing vegetables could be described as an art form in the Middle East as almost every vegetable is stuffed with meat or rice and they all look fabulous. Believed to have originated in the Topkapı kitchens during the Ottoman Empire, these stuffed vegetables are called 'dolma' in Turkey (where the same word, dolmuş is the name for a stuffed taxi!), 'dolmeh' in Iran and 'mahshi' to the Arabs of the Middle East. Some stuffed vegetables can be very elaborate and fiddly to make, such as the long, slender aubergines/eggplants, which are hollowed out by pummelling and squeezing so that they remain intact, and most vegetables are stuffed with an aromatic pilaf made with short-grain rice or bulgur, or with a combination of meat and rice. Variations of this traditional recipe, 'makshi basal', can be found throughout Iran, Turkey, Syria, Jordan, Israel and the Palestinian Territories. Large golden or red onions are ideal for this dish as the layers can be easily unravelled, stuffed and rolled up again.

2–3 big onions, peeled and left whole

250 g/9 oz. lean minced/ground lamb

90 g/scant ½ cup long-grain rice, rinsed and drained

1 tablespoon tomato purée/paste

2 teaspoons ground cinnamon

1 teaspoon ground allspice

1 teaspoon ground cumin

1 teaspoon ground coriander

a small bunch of fresh flat-leaf parsley, finely chopped

sea salt and freshly ground black pepper

2–3 tablespoons olive oil

1–2 tablespoons tamarind paste

1 tablespoon runny honey

roughly 150 ml/⅔ cup water

1 tablespoon butter

Serves 4–6

Preheat the oven to 200°C (400°F) Gas 6.

Bring a saucepan of water to the boil. Cut each onion down one side from the top to the bottom and pop them into the boiling water for about 10 minutes, until they are soft and begin to unravel. Drain and refresh the onions and separate the layers.

In a bowl, pound the lamb mince, slapping it down into the bowl to eliminate any air pockets. Add the rice, tomato paste/purée, spices, most of the parsley and seasoning and knead well, making sure it is thoroughly mixed together.

Spread the onion layers out on a clean surface and place a spoonful of the meat mixture into each one. Roll them up loosely, leaving room for the rice to expand on cooking. Tuck in the ends and pack the stuffed onions close together in a heavy-based pan. Mix together the olive oil, tamarind paste and honey with the water and pour it over the stuffed onions.

Cover the pan with a lid or aluminium foil and pop it in the preheated oven for about 20 minutes, until the rice has expanded. Take the lid or foil off the onions, dot their tops with a little butter and place them back in the oven, uncovered for 15–20 minutes, until nicely browned on top and slightly caramelized. Remove them from the oven and serve immediately.

Spices and herbs

There is a certain magic to the Middle Eastern spice souks, bazaars and open markets, which lure you with their enticing aroma of roasted nuts and seeds, the kaleidoscope of brightly coloured, powdered dyes for food, hair and clothing, freshly picked herbs tied in bunches like flowers, crates of gleaming vegetables and fruit, and the fascinating collections of native barks, seeds, reptile skins and beetles to be ground as mystical remedies or aphrodisiacs. There is nothing quite like the hustle and bustle of haggling and shopping amongst the incense, heady perfumes, aromatic flavourings and endless offerings of tea or coffee and, whether it's in the medieval labrynthine spice streets of ancient cities or in the rural markets amongst the mules, camels and livestock, you become enveloped in the long history of trade that has taken place across this vast region.

The geographical positions of Arabia and Persia played a pivotal role in the spice trade long before the advent of Islam as they acted as transit points for both the land and the sea spice routes from East to West. During the Crusades, trading posts were established far and wide; Arabs and Persian merchants acted as the first middlemen but were replaced by the Jews and the Syrians. Spices were transported on the backs of camels across the Arabian Desert to Palestine and Syria and by boat via Cairo on their way to Constantinople, Genoa and Venice.

Indigenous spices, such as coriander/cilantro and cumin, marry well with both the spices heralding from the Spice Islands (an archipelago now part of modern-day Indonesia), like cinnamon, cloves and nutmeg, and with the more recent chillies/chiles and allspice, which were brought from the New World in the 16th century by the Spaniards who traded with the Ottomans. As the ancient yin and yang theories of China filtered through to the Middle East during the Seljuk and Ottoman periods, a belief in balancing the warming and cooling properties of certain foods developed. This was achieved by adding 'warm' spices and herbs to 'cool' vegetables and pulses and the belief is still evident in the foundations of modern Middle Eastern cooking. Warming spices such as cumin, cinnamon and cloves are believed to induce the appetite and aid digestion and they are often combined with garlic, which is believed to be beneficial to the circulation of the blood.

The dried red chilli/chile pepper is the most remarkable spice of all. It is the most ubiquitous spice in the Middle East, yet it is one of the newest. Cultivated in every corner of the region, fresh green and red chillies/chiles of varying shapes and sizes are widely used in salads and grilled dishes but it is the dried red chilli/chile that is employed as a spice. The small, thin red chillies/chiles and the long, horn-shaped ones are dried and hung on strings in markets, gardens, terraces and balconies. Sold whole, finely chopped or ground to a powder, this dried red chilli/chile pepper fits so snugly into Middle Eastern cooking you would think that it had been there since ancient times.

The most expensive spice is saffron — literally worth its weight in gold as it is the only spice in the world to be measured by the carat. Cultivated in Turkey and Morocco, saffron is the dye contained in the dried stigmas of the purple crocus, which only flowers for two weeks in October. Roughly 10,000 crocus heads need to be picked to yield a mere 50 g/2 oz. of saffron, which explains its price. The mildly perfumed stigmas are usually sold in small quantities, often in a tangle of burnt-orangey-red threads, and come to life when soaked in water or milk, imparting a magnificent yellow dye with a hint of floral notes. Needless to say, it's only used for special occasions.

In Middle Eastern cooking, spices go hand in hand with herbs. Generous quantities of parsley, mint and dill are often combined as a traditional warming triad to balance the cooling properties of some vegetables and pulses/beans. Parsley is eaten to heighten the appetite or temper the flavours, and small bunches of parsley always accompany fiery dishes with the idea that you chew on the leaves to cut the spice. Along with parsley, mint is the most used herb, both fresh and dried. It is added liberally to yogurt dips, mezze dishes and salads, and it is brewed in tea. Fresh coriander/cilantro is commonly used in North Africa and in Arab cooking, whereas dill is a great favourite in Turkish and Lebanese dishes. Other popular herbs include sage, which is widely used in vegetable and meat dishes, and the dried leafy stalks are tied in thick bundles destined for an aromatic winter tea; fresh and dried oregano, which is a favourite herb to sprinkle over roasted or grilled lamb; thyme or 'mountain oregano' which plays a particular role in dishes prepared with sheep's tail fat as the herb is believed to cut the fat and aid digestion, and the dried sprigs, are brewed in a herbal tea that is drunk as an aphrodisiac.

Chicken, onions and sumac with pitta bread

This simple and tasty snack was first introduced to me as a Palestinian peasant dish and, although I have enjoyed several variations since then, it is the Palestinian version that has remained in my memory. 'Musakhan' is a popular dish in Jordan where there is a huge Palestinian community and it is often only considered authentic if it is prepared with the traditional 'taboon' bread — flat, spongy loaves, which are baked on stones placed on the floor of the village communal, outdoor, clay oven. Like the 'fatta' dishes of Syria and Lebanon, the bread is often employed as a base for ensuing layered ingredients but musakhan can also be prepared with a layer of bread at the base and one on top, like a large club sandwich or an open pie, and they are often served as a tasty and tangy street snack by tucking the ingredients into the hollow pouch of toasted pitta bread, which is an easy way to enjoy it at home.

2 tablespoons Samna (page 13), or 2 tablespoons olive oil with a knob/pat of butter

2 onions, sliced

2—3 garlic cloves, crushed

700 g/1¾ lbs. chicken breasts, cut into bite-size strips

2—3 teaspoons ground sumac

1 teaspoon crushed cardamom seeds

1—2 teaspoons baharat mix

freshly squeezed juice of 1 unwaxed lemon

2 tablespoons toasted pine nuts

a small bunch of fresh flat-leaf parsley, finely chopped

sea salt and freshly ground black pepper

4 pitta breads, halved crossways to form 8 pockets

4 generous tablespoons thick, creamy yogurt

baking sheet, lightly oiled

Serves 4

Preheat the oven to 180°C (350°F) Gas 4.

Heat the samna, or olive oil and butter in a heavy-based pan and stir in the onions. When they begin to soften, add the garlic and fry until the onions turn golden brown.

Add the chicken and cook for 2—3 minutes, before stirring in most of the sumac, cardamom and baharat mix. Add the lemon juice and cook gently until the chicken is tender but still juicy. Toss in most of the pine nuts and parsley and season to taste with salt and pepper.

Place the pitta halves on the prepared baking sheet. Pop them in the preheated oven for about 10 minutes to toast them. Fill the toasted pouches with the chicken mixture, top each one with a dollop of yogurt and scatter the reserved sumac, pine nuts and parsley over the top. Serve immediately as a tasty snack.

Chicken tagine with ginger, green olives and preserved lemon

Tagines are an invention of the Berbers, the indigenous people of Morocco. The word is used to describe both the earthenware cooking vessel with its conical lid and the dish that is cooked in it. The Berbers lived in North Africa, between Egypt and the western coast of Morocco, as far back as archaeological records go. As a result, they have had a culinary influence on the region, such as their splendidly succulent tagines. Mainly farmers by tradition, they have lived alongside the nomadic Touareg and Bedouins of the desert and, even after the Arab invasion and the forced conversion to Islam, the Berbers have managed to hold on to their culinary traditions. **This chicken tagine features two of Morocco's classic ingredients — cracked green olives and preserved lemons.**

3 garlic cloves, crushed

a bunch of fresh coriander/cilantro, finely chopped, plus extra to garnish

freshly squeezed juice of 1 unwaxed lemon

1 teaspoon sea salt

1 whole organic chicken, roughly 1.3 kg/ 2¾ lbs. in weight

3—4 tablespoons olive oil

1 large onion, grated

a generous pinch of saffron fronds/threads

40 g/1½ oz. piece of fresh ginger, peeled and grated

1 teaspoon freshly ground black pepper

2 cinnamon sticks

2 teaspoons coriander seeds

175 g/1 generous cup cracked green olives

the rind of 1 preserved lemon, cut into thin strips

25 g/2 tablespoons butter

1—2 tablespoons runny honey

Serves 4—6

Rub the garlic, most of the coriander/cilantro, lemon juice and salt into the cavity of the chicken. Mix together the olive oil with the grated onion, saffron, ginger and pepper and rub the mixture over the outside of the chicken. Cover and leave to stand for about 30 minutes.

Place the chicken in a large tagine or in a heavy-based casserole pot. Pour the marinade juices over it and add enough water to come almost half way up the chicken. Add the cinnamon sticks and coriander seeds and bring the water to the boil. Reduce the heat, cover with the lid and simmer for about 1 hour, turning the chicken over from time to time.

Preheat the oven to 180°C (350°F) Gas 4.

Lift the chicken out of the tagine or casserole pot and place it on a board. Quickly, turn up the heat and boil the cooking liquid to reduce it. Stir in the olives and preserved lemon and keep reducing the liquid until it just covers the base of the tagine. Season the cooking juices to taste.

Place the chicken back into the tagine, baste it thoroughly with the cooking juices, dot the top of the chicken with bits of butter and drizzle with the honey. Roast the chicken for 15—20 minutes in the preheated oven until it is golden-brown. Garnish it with coriander/cilantro and serve immediately with crusty bread or couscous to mop up the tangy, buttery juices.

Char-grilled quails with currants, green peppercorns and pomegranate seeds

This is a simple and tasty way of cooking and eating small birds, such as quails, poussins and pigeons. Popular street food in Turkey, the eastern Mediterranean and right across North Africa, they make a delicious snack tucked into a half loaf of flat or leavened bread, topped with onions, parsley and sumac. The aroma of the marinated birds grilling on a spit over hot charcoal invariably lures you over to the stall or café to have a look and a taste. To grill the birds, they are 'butterflied'; first by splitting then down the backbone and laying them flat. They are then usually marinated in the juice of sour pomegranates as it tenderizes the meat as well as enhances the flavour, but you can use the juice of sweet pomegranates mixed with a little tart lemon juice or sumac.

4 quails, cleaned and boned (you can ask your butcher to do this)

4 fresh pomegranates, squeezed for juice

freshly squeezed juice of 1 unwaxed lemon or 2 teaspoons ground sumac

2 tablespoons olive oil

1–2 teaspoons finely chopped dried red chilli/chile or paprika

2–3 tablespoons thick, creamy yogurt

sea salt and freshly ground black pepper

a bunch of fresh flat–leaf parsley

1–2 tablespoons Samna (page 13), or
1–2 tablespoons olive oil with a knob/pat of butter

1 tablespoon dried currants

1–2 teaspoons pickled green peppercorns

the seeds of half a pomegranate

8 wooden skewers, soaked in water for 15 minutes

charcoal grill or barbecue

Serves 4

First, thread one skewer through the wings of each bird and a second skewer through the legs to keep them together. Place the trussed birds in a wide, shallow bowl or dish. Beat the pomegranate juice with the lemon juice or sumac, olive oil and chopped chilli/chile. Pour the mixture over the quails, rubbing it into the skin. Cover with foil and leave the birds to marinate in the refrigerator for 2–3 hours, turning them from time to time.

Prepare the barbecue for cooking. Lift the birds out of the marinade and pour what is left of it into a bowl. Beat the yogurt into the leftover marinade and add a little salt and pepper. Brush some of the thick yogurt mixture over the birds and place them on the barbecue. Cook them for 4–5 minutes each side, brushing with yogurt as they cook to form a crust.

Finely chop a little of the parsley and put aside for garnishing. Arrange the rest of the parsley on a serving dish. Place the cooked quails on top of it. Quickly heat the samna, or olive oil and butter in a frying pan/skillet and stir in the currants and green peppercorns until the currants plump up, then spoon the mixture over the quails. Garnish them with the rest of the parsley and pomegranate seeds and serve with a pilaf or flatbread, yogurt and a salad.

fish and seafood

Poached fish with saffron rice and caviar

This popular Arab dish, 'sayyadiah', varies from region to region in the Middle East. Originally a simple way of preparing the day's catch, the dish has become more sophisticated over time; particularly in Lebanon where it often features on menus or is cooked in the home as a special dish to honour guests. This recipe combines several different versions of sayyadiah that I have tasted in Egypt and the Levant, where it has occasionally been prepared with smoked fish and spices. I have garnished it with caviar from the Caspian Sea where the fishing communities prepare a similar dish with the local sturgeon.

600 ml/2½ cups fish stock or water

sea salt and freshly ground black pepper

a pinch of saffron fronds/threads

450 g/2¼ cups long-grain rice, well rinsed and drained

a bunch of fresh flat-leaf parsley

900 g/2 lbs. firm-fleshed, boned, plain and smoked fish fillets, such as sea bass or trout combined with smoked haddock

6 black peppercorns

2–3 fresh bay leaves

1 cinnamon stick

1 tablespoon Samna (page 13), or 1 tablespoon olive oil with a knob/pat of butter

2 onions, finely sliced

1 teaspoon cumin seeds

2 teaspoons coriander seeds

2 teaspoons finely chopped dried red chilli/chile

2 tablespoons pine nuts

4–6 teaspoons black or red caviar, to serve

1 unwaxed lemon, cut into wedges, to serve

Serves 4–6

Pour the stock into a heavy-based pan and bring it to the boil. Season the stock with salt and pepper and stir in the saffron fronds/threads and rice. Continue to boil vigorously for 3–4 minutes, then reduce the heat and simmer for about 10–15 minutes, until all the liquid has been absorbed. Turn off the heat, cover the pan with a clean tea/dish towel, put on the lid and leave the rice to steam for 10 minutes.

Meanwhile, line a heavy-based pan with the parsley and place the fish fillets on top. Scatter the peppercorns, bay leaves and cinnamon sticks over and around the fish and pour in enough water to just cover the fillets. Bring the water to the boil, reduce the heat and simmer gently for 5 minutes. Turn off the heat and cover the pan to keep the fish warm and moist.

Heat the samna, or olive oil and butter and stir in the onions, cumin and coriander seeds for 3–4 minutes, until the onions begin to turn golden in colour. Quickly dry roast the pine nuts in a frying pan/skillet until they begin to brown and emit a nutty aroma, then tip them into a bowl.

Tip the rice onto a serving dish and toss most of the onions and spices through it. Break up the fish with your fingers, stir some of it through the rice and arrange the rest on top. Scatter the rest of the onions over the fish and sprinkle the pine nuts and the rest of the chopped chilli/chile over the top.

To finish off the dish, garnish with a little mound of caviar around the edge of the dish and lemon wedges to squeeze over the fish.

Pan-fried red mullet with pink peppercorns, currants and tahini sauce

150 ml/⅔ cup smooth tahini

freshly squeezed juice of 1 unwaxed lemon

grated zest and freshly squeezed juice of
1 orange

3 garlic cloves

sea salt and freshly ground black pepper

2–3 teaspoons pink peppercorns

a bunch of fresh flat-leaf parsley, finely
chopped

4 fresh red mullet, small red snapper or
sea bass, gutted, cleaned and patted dry

2 tablespoons plain/all-purpose flour

2 tablespoons Samna (page 13), or
2 tablespoons olive oil with a knob/pat
of butter

1–2 tablespoons (Zante) currants

1 unwaxed lemon, quartered, to serve

Serves 4

Fish have played a significant role in the Middle East since antiquity — they have been carved into the walls of early tombs and depicted on murals as well as in metal and jewellery; they have traditionally been a symbol of Christianity; the Jews display a fish head in the centre of the table to indicate that they will always be at the 'head'; the Iranians eat fish at New Year to cleanse their bodies of evil; and there is a widespread belief that fish ward off the evil eye. The type of fish employed for different dishes is rarely specified but, in the eastern Mediterranean and in Turkey, red mullet is regarded as a fish of distinction as it is much sought-after for its splendidly pink colouring and succulent flesh, making it ideal for grilling and frying whole. If red mullet isn't available, try red snapper or sea bass instead.

First prepare the tahini sauce. Beat the tahini paste in a bowl with the lemon and orange juices, until the mixture is thick and smooth with the consistency of pouring cream. Crush 2 of the garlic cloves, beat them into the tahini and season to taste with salt and pepper. Spoon the tahini sauce into a serving bowl and put aside.

Using a pestle and mortar, crush half the pink peppercorns with the remaining garlic clove, the orange zest and 1 tablespoon of the chopped parsley to form a thick paste. Slash 3 shallow, diagonal cuts into each side of the fish with a sharp knife. Rub the pink peppercorn paste into the cuts and sprinkle the fish with salt. Toss them in the flour so that they are lightly coated.

Heat the samna, or olive oil and butter in a heavy-based pan and cook the fish for about 3 minutes on each side, until they are crisp and golden. Drain the fish on paper towels and arrange them on a serving dish.

Add the rest of the peppercorns and the (Zante) currants to the pan and cook until the currants plump up. Spoon them over the fish, and garnish with the parsley. Serve immediately with the lemon wedges and the tahini sauce.

Fish cakes with apricots, sunflower seeds and cinnamon

450 g/1 lb. fresh or cooked fish fillets such as sea bass, sea bream or haddock

2 slices day-old bread, soaked in a little water and squeezed dry

1 red onion, finely chopped

2 tablespoons dried apricots, finely chopped

2 tablespoons toasted sunflower seeds

1 teaspoon ground cumin

1 teaspoon ground coriander

2 teaspoons ground cinnamon

2 teaspoons tomato purée/paste or ketchup

1 egg, lightly beaten

sea salt and freshly ground black pepper

2 small bunches of fresh flat-leaf parsley, finely chopped, reserving half to serve

a small bunch of fresh dill, finely chopped

a small bunch of fresh mint, finely chopped

3–4 tablespoons plain/all-purpose flour

3–4 tablespoons sunflower oil, for frying

a dusting of cinnamon, to serve

1–2 unwaxed lemons or limes, cut into wedges, to serve

Serves 4

Served as a snack in the street or in a café, as a hot mezze dish or as a main course, fish cakes are versatile and tasty and a perfect vehicle for fusing the flavours of the different regions. For a Moroccan version you can spike them with Harissa (page 14); in the Arabian Gulf, you might find them flavoured with zhug, baharat spice mix or powdered dried limes; and in the Levant, they are often flavoured with herbs and warming spices like cumin and cinnamon and combined with dried fruit and nuts. Similarly, you can prepare fish kibbeh, combining the ingredients with bulgur in the tradition of the Lebanese and Syrian speciality, which is often prepared in Christian communities for Lent.

In a bowl, break up the fish fillets with a fork. Add the bread, onion, apricots, sunflower seeds and spices. Add the tomato purée/paste and the egg and season well with salt and pepper. Toss in the fresh herbs and, using your hands, knead the fish cake ingredients together and mould the mixture into circular shapes, about 2 cm/¾ in. thick.

Tip the flour onto a plate. Take each ball in your hand and gently press it in your palm to flatten it a little into a thick disc-shaped cake. Roll each fish cake lightly in the flour.

Heat the sunflower oil in a wide shallow pan and fry the fish cakes in batches, until golden brown on both sides. Drain them on paper towels. Dust with a little cinnamon, garnish with the parsley and serve hot with the lemon or lime wedges to squeeze over them.

Fish tagine with cabbage and chermoula

The fish tagines of Morocco's coastal areas, such as Tangier and Casablanca, are redolent with spices and buttery sauces, often piquant with lemon and chillies/chiles and tempered with fresh herbs. The fish is cooked to perfection and remains juicy and moist in the earthenware dish with its conical lid. The distinct Moroccan coriander-/cilantro-based marinade, chermoula, is often employed in the fish dishes of North Africa and influences the local dishes of places at the other end of the Mediterranean, such as Egypt, Jordan and Lebanon. You can use any firm-fleshed fish for this tagine; serve it with chunks of fresh bread to mop up the buttery lemon and coriander/cilantro juices.

2–3 garlic cloves, chopped

1 fresh red chilli/chile, seeded and chopped

1 teaspoon sea salt

a small bunch of fresh coriander/cilantro

a pinch of saffron fronds/threads

1–2 teaspoons ground cumin

3–4 tablespoons olive oil

freshly squeezed juice of 1 unwaxed lemon

1 kg/2¼ lbs. fresh monkfish tail or a firm-fleshed fish, cut into large chunks

2–3 tablespoons olive oil

2 onions, finely sliced

half a green cabbage, finely sliced or shredded

1 preserved lemon, finely chopped (page 16)

a 400-g/14.5-oz. can plum tomatoes, drained of juice

1–2 teaspoons granulated sugar

500 ml/2 cups fish stock or water

sea salt and freshly ground black pepper

a bunch of fresh mint leaves, finely shredded

Serves 4–6

First make the chermoula using a pestle and mortar. Pound the garlic and chilli/chile with the salt to form a paste. Add the coriander/cilantro leaves and pound to a coarse paste. Beat in the saffron and cumin and bind well with the olive oil and lemon juice. Reserve 2 teaspoons of chermoula for cooking and coat the fish in the rest. Cover and leave to marinate in the refrigerator for 1–2 hours.

Heat the oil in the base of a tagine or a heavy-based pan. Stir in the onion for 2 minutes to soften then add the cabbage for 2–3 minutes. Stir in most of the preserved lemon with the reserved 2 teaspoons of chermoula and add the tomatoes with the sugar. Pour in the stock, bring it to the boil, then reduce the heat and simmer for 10–15 minutes with the lid on.

Season the stock to taste then slip the marinated fish into the tagine. Cover with the lid and cook gently for about 4–5 minutes, until the fish is cooked through. Garnish the tagine with the reserved preserved lemon and the shredded mint and serve with chunks of crusty bread, rice or couscous.

Char-grilled fish with harissa and a date coating

In the early cookery manuals of the eastern Mediterranean, recipes rarely specified the type of fish to be used. This was probably because people tended to use whatever fish was available and, in the case of Jordan and Iraq, that was more likely to be of the freshwater variety. When you look at the whole of the Middle East, though, there is an extensive coastline and several different seas to choose from. These seas yield bountiful catches of sea bass, red snapper, garfish, hake, grouper, sardines, swordfish, tuna, grey and red mullet (the latter being a fish that was favoured by the Romans), and sole, 'samak Moussa', which is named after Moses as it is believed that when he separated the Red Sea this particular fish was cut in half and remained thin for evermore. The culinary destination for most of these fish is a good grilling over charcoal, 'samak mashwi', of which there are some interesting variations such as this traditional Bedouin one – popular in Oman, Saudi Arabia, Jordan and Iraq as the coating of puréed dates imparts a delicious fruity flavour to the fish.

250 g/1⅔ cups fresh pitted/stoned dates

1 onion, finely chopped

2 garlic cloves, crushed

1 teaspoon ground turmeric

1–2 teaspoons Harissa (page 14)

1 fairly large trout or sea bass, gutted and cleaned (don't remove the scales)

sea salt

a few sprigs of fresh flat-leaf parsley

charcoal grill/barbecue

Serves 4

Prepare the charcoal grill.

Put the dates in a blender or a food processor with 1–2 tablespoons of water to form a smooth purée – if your dates are not moist they will need to be soaked in water for several hours first.

In a small bowl, mix together the onion, garlic, turmeric and harissa. Rub the mixture around the inside of the fish, sprinkle with a little salt and lay a few sprigs of parsley in the cavity too. Seal the cavity with a thin metal skewer, by weaving it through the two sides of the cavity.

Push a long skewer through the mouth of the fish and stand it in a jug/pitcher to support it or stab the protruding end into the ground. Make sure the skin of the fish is dry then rub the sticky date purée over it. Leave the fish to sit for about 10–15 minutes, so that the date purée firms up a little.

When the grill is ready, hold the fish above the charcoal and cook for about 5 minutes on each side. When serving, peel back the date-encrusted skin to reveal the succulent fruity flesh.

Char-grilled sardines in vine leaves with tomatoes

The most popular method of cooking fish in the Middle East is to grill it over charcoal. Undoubtedly, it is the simplest and most enjoyable way to eat fresh fish as nothing quite beats the aroma and taste of cooking over a charcoal grill in the open air. The tangy, charred vine leaves in this recipe are a perfect partner for the oilier flesh of sardines, mackerel, red mullet or large anchovies. In all the markets along the eastern Mediterranean coast you will find stacks of fresh vine leaves or jars of preserved leaves, destined for dishes like this. If you are using fresh leaves, simply plunge them into boiling water for a couple of minutes to soften them – the bright green leaves will deepen in colour – then drain and refresh them before using them in the recipe. For vine leaves that are preserved in brine, you need to soak them for 10–15 minutes in a bowl of boiling water to remove the salt, then drain, refresh and pat them dry.

4 tablespoons olive oil

freshly squeezed juice of 1 unwaxed lemon

1 tablespoon balsamic or white wine vinegar

1–2 teaspoons of honey

1 red chilli/chile, seeded and finely chopped

a few fresh dill fronds/threads, finely chopped

a few sprigs of fresh flat-leaf parsley, finely chopped

sea salt and freshly ground black pepper

8–12 fresh sardines, with the scales removed, gutted and thoroughly washed

2 tablespoons olive oil

freshly squeezed juice of half an unwaxed lemon

8–12 vine leaves, prepared as above

sea salt

olive oil, for brushing

4 fresh vine tomatoes, halved or quartered

charcoal grill/barbecue

Serves 4

In a bowl, mix together all the ingredients for the dressing. Season to taste with salt and pepper and put aside.

Place the sardines in a flat dish. In a bowl, mix together the olive oil and lemon juice and brush it lightly over the sardines. Put aside for 15 minutes.

Meanwhile, prepare the charcoal grill/barbecue until just right for grilling. Spread the vine leaves on a flat surface and place a sardine on each leaf. Sprinkle each one with a little salt and wrap loosely in the leaf, like a cigar with the tail and head poking out. Brush each leaf with a little olive oil and place it seam-side down on a plate. Sprinkle the tomatoes with a little salt too. Transfer both the sardines and the tomatoes to the barbecue and cook on each side for 3–4 minutes, until the vine leaves are charred and the tomatoes are soft and slightly charred too.

Transfer the barbecued sardines to a serving dish and arrange the tomatoes around them. Drizzle the dressing over the whole lot and serve immediately, while still hot.

Religious Customs and Traditions

The most prominent language in the Middle East is Arabic. Other principal languages include Farsi, Hebrew, Turkish, and French, as well as many local dialects and tribal tongues. The principal religion in the Middle East is Islam, so it exerts the most influence on the customs, traditions and culinary cultures of the region. The principal book of Islam is the Qur'an, which is written Arabic and is a collection of revelations or commands from God (Allah) received by the Prophet Muhammad through the Angel Gabriel. Muhammad recited these messages to his companions and followers who wrote them down on a piece of cloth, a stone — any object they could find — and they were copied and preserved after Muhammad's death and compiled later in a series of Sutras, the chapters of the Qur'an.

Muhammad mentioned food many times in his recitations, repeating in particular the kinds of foods that were permitted or forbidden, thus laying the foundation for Muslim dietary laws which are religiously carried out to this day. These laws include the

prohibition of alcohol, although this is observed in varying degrees of laxity in different communities, and the slaughtering and consumption of meat: the animal must be alive and slaughtered by cutting its throat; the blood must not be consumed; an animal slaughtered for any other God or pagan deity is forbidden; an animal that is killed for any reason other than food, or is already dead, is forbidden; and no part of the pig is permitted. There is also a law for the slaughterer, who must turn the head of the animal toward Mecca and utter the words: 'In the name of God, God is most great.'

Similarly, Jews adhere to the dietary laws of kashrut, which were revealed to Moses on Mount Sinai. These detailed laws also spell out what is permitted, or kosher, and what is not, particularly regarding the slaughtering and cooking of animals: only those that 'chew the cud' and have cloven hooves are permitted; the animals must be slaughtered by cutting the throat and draining the blood; the consumption of blood is forbidden so all traces of it have to be removed to render it kosher by

soaking the meat in cold water and sprinkling it with salt to draw out the blood before washing it clean three times in cold water.

Outside the Christian communities of the Middle East, it is rare for pork to be consumed. The preferred meat is mutton or lamb, followed by beef and veal. Goats, water buffaloes, and camels are also eaten in some communities but the most highly prized meat comes from the ancient fat-tailed sheep, which stores fat in its tail as a reserve in arid climates. Ever since the early nomads herded their sheep, this tail fat has been coveted as a delicacy and is used as a source of cooking fuel.

For ritual slaughters, such as religious feasts, births, funerals and weddings, sheep and goats are the animals of choice and they are either cooked whole on a spit, or divided up into different cuts to be used in a variety of traditional dishes: the tail is boiled and eaten with bread; the intestines are stuffed with offal and spices and grilled, or simmered in soup; the head is usually boiled in soup and the eyes served as a delicacy; the brains are boiled separately and eaten cold with lemon or vinegar; the feet are boiled and served on bread with yogurt; and the rest of the meat is either roasted or cooked in stews.

One of the religious traditions shared by Muslims and Jews is the near-sacrifice of Isma'il (Isaac in the Bible) by his father, Ibrahim (Abraham). To mark this occasion, Jews bake a sheep's head in the oven to signify the ram that Abraham saw and sacrificed instead. Muslims, on the other hand, mark the event with a festival called Eid-el-Kurban in which sheep are led through the streets and villages to be sold to those who can afford one to take home and slaughter for the ensuing ceremonial feast.

Another religious custom that Muslims must adhere to is the month of Ramadan, the ninth month on the Islamic lunar calendar. This is the month that Muslims abstain from food and drink between sunrise and sunset. This act of self-discipline reminds Muslims to submit themselves completely to the will of God and to think of the poor who are frequently without food. In preparation for each day of fasting, a meal is laid out just before sunrise and the second one of the day is enjoyed just after the sun has set. The month of fasting comes to a joyous end when the new moon emerges and a three-day feast, Eid al-Fitr begins with great merriment and an exchange of gifts.

Fish stew with tamarind, hilbeh and dried limes

This deliciously sour and spicy stew is most commonly found in Jordan, Egypt, Yemen, Oman, the United Arab Emirates and Kuwait as both the sweet and sour limes grow in this region. The sour limes, 'limun baladi', are dried whole to impart a musty, tangy flavour to dishes, particularly fish stews and soups. The other flavours of this dish, which can be prepared with fish steaks or large prawns/shrimp, echo the history of trade between the Arabs and the Indians – tamarind, turmeric, fenugreek and fresh coriander/cilantro. Hilbeh is a distinctive paste from the Arabian Gulf made with fenugreek seeds that have been soaked in water until they form a jelly-like coating and are then pounded with garlic, chilli/chile and fresh coriander/cilantro. Dried tamarind pulp, dried limes or powdered dried lime and hilbeh are available in Middle Eastern stores.

120 g/4 oz. dried tamarind pulp, soaked in 350 ml/1½ cups hot water for 20 minutes

1–2 tablespoons olive oil

1 kg/2 lbs. 4oz. fish steaks, such as sea bream, grouper or sea bass

1 onion, halved and sliced

3–4 garlic cloves, chopped

40 g/1½ oz. piece of fresh ginger, peeled and chopped

2 teaspoons ground turmeric

2–3 dried limes, pierced twice with a skewer

1–2 teaspoons hilbeh paste

roughly 12 small new potatoes, peeled and left whole

a 400-g/14.5-oz. can plum tomatoes, drained of juice

2 teaspoons granulated or palm sugar

sea salt and freshly ground black pepper

a bunch of fresh coriander/cilantro, finely chopped

1 unwaxed lemon, cut into wedges, to serve

Serves 4–6

Squeeze the tamarind pulp in your hand to separate the pulp from the seeds and stalks then strain the pulp through a sieve/strainer. Reserve the strained liquid.

Heat the oil in a heavy based pan and sear the fish steaks for 1–2 minutes on each side then transfer them to a plate. Stir the onion, garlic and ginger into the pan until they begin to colour. Add the turmeric, dried limes and hilbeh then toss in the potatoes and cook for 2–3 minutes. Stir in the tomatoes with the sugar, pour in the strained tamarind liquid and bring the liquid to the boil. Reduce the heat, cover the pan and simmer gently for about 15 minutes, until the potatoes are tender.

Season with salt and pepper to taste then slip in the seared fish steaks. Cover the pan again and cook gently for about 10 minutes, until the fish is cooked. Toss half the coriander/cilantro in the stew and use the rest to garnish the dish. Serve hot with rice and lemon wedges to squeeze over the fish.

Anchovies and rice in a dome

This classic Turkish rice dish with anchovies, 'hamsili pilav', is from the Black Sea coast, where anchovies are used in many dishes and written about with passion in song and poetry. Along with hazelnuts and tea, it is what the Black Sea region is famous for — anchovy madness. Packed full of anchovies, there are several ways of making this dish — whole anchovies can be fried and tossed through the rice; the anchovies and rice can be layered and baked in the oven; or the anchovies can be boned and used to line an oven dish to form a mould in which the rice is baked. The third option is the most impressive to look at and is enjoyable to eat because there are no bones. The striking dome should be served as a course on its own to appreciate the work that goes into it and the significance of the little anchovy.

600 g/1¼ lbs. fresh anchovies, with heads, guts and backbones removed

sea salt

2 tablespoons Samna (page 13), or 2 tablespoons olive oil with a knob/pat of butter

1 onion, finely chopped

2 tablespoons pine nuts

1 tablespoon dried mint

1 teaspoon ground allspice

450 g/2¼ cups long-grain rice, thoroughly rinsed and drained

freshly ground black pepper

a small bunch of fresh dill, finely chopped, with a few fronds reserved for garnishing

1 unwaxed lemon, cut into wedges, to serve

dome-shaped ovenproof dish

Serves 4–6

Preheat the oven to 180°C (350°F) Gas 4.

Rinse the anchovies and pat them dry. Open them out like butterflies and sprinkle with salt. Lightly grease a dome-shaped oven dish or an ovenproof bowl and line it with the butterflied anchovies, skin-side down, to form a mould for the rice. Reserve some anchovies for the top.

Heat the samna, or olive oil and butter in a heavy based pan. Stir in the onion and cook until it softens. Add the pine nuts and cook until golden. Stir in the mint, allspice and rice, and season with salt and pepper. Pour in enough water to just cover the rice (roughly 2 cm/¾ in, above the rice grains) and bring it to the boil. Reduce the heat and simmer until the water has been absorbed. Turn off the heat, sprinkle the dill over the rice, cover with a clean tea/dish towel, followed by the lid and leave to steam for 10 minutes.

Fluff up the rice with a fork to mix in the dill and tip it into the anchovy mould. Lay the remaining anchovies, skin-side up this time, over the top of the rice. Splash a little water over the top and place the dish in the preheated oven for about 20 minutes.

When ready to serve, invert a serving plate over the top of the dish. With one hand, hold the bottom-side of the serving dish, and use the other to turn the ovenproof dish upside down. Carefully slip off the ovenproof dish to reveal the anchovy mould encasing the rice. Garnish with the dill fronds and serve immediately with the lemon to squeeze over it.

Spicy grilled squid with hummus and pine nuts

FOR THE MARINADE

2 teaspoons cumin seeds, roasted

1 teaspoon coriander seeds, roasted

1 teaspoon black peppercorns

2—3 garlic cloves, crushed

sea salt

grated zest of 1 unwaxed lemon

1 tablespoon dried sage leaves, crumbled

2—3 tablespoons olive oil

8 baby squid

olive oil, for brushing

1—2 tablespoons pine nuts

a dusting of paprika

a small bunch of fresh flat-leaf parsley, finely chopped

1 unwaxed lemon, cut into wedges, to serve

FOR THE HUMMUS

1 x 400-g/14.5-oz. can chickpeas, rinsed and drained

freshly squeezed juice of 1 unwaxed lemon

1—2 garlic cloves

1 teaspoon cumin seeds

3—4 tablespoons olive oil

sea salt and freshly ground black pepper

ridged stovetop pan

Serves 4

The abundance and size of the shellfish along the coastline of the eastern Mediterranean, the Red Sea, the Arabian Sea and the Gulf can be quite spectacular. There is a regional preference for large prawns/jumbo shrimp that are ideal for grilling, large mussels that the Ottomans loved to stuff with aromatic rice and squid which is usually grilled or fried in batter in the manner of the well-known Mediterranean kalamari. Shellfish also lends itself to fusion recipes such as this one, which I have tasted in Dubai, Cairo and Istanbul.

To prepare the squid, hold the body sac in one hand and pull the head off with the other. Most of the innards should come out with the head, but reach inside the sac with your fingers to remove any that remain in there. Whip out the transparent backbone and rinse the body sac inside and out. Pat the body sac dry. Sever the tentacles just above the eyes, so that you have the top of the head and the tentacle joined together. Put them aside with the sacs and discard everything else.

Now make the marinade. Using a pestle and mortar, pound the roasted cumin and coriander seeds with the peppercorns. Beat in the crushed garlic, salt, lemon zest and sage leaves. Then, bind with the olive oil.

Using a sharp knife, score the squid sacs in a criss-cross pattern and rub them and the tentacles with the spicy marinade. Set aside to marinade for 30 minutes.

Meanwhile, prepare the hummus. Put the chickpeas into a blender or a food processor with the lemon juice, garlic and cumin seeds and blend to a thick paste. Drizzle in the olive oil while you blend, until the hummus is thick and creamy. Season with salt and pepper to taste, tip it into a small saucepan, and heat it up slowly, stirring from time to time.

Heat a ridged stovetop pan and dry roast the pine nuts. Tip them onto a plate, return the pan to the heat and brush it with a little oil. Place the marinated sacs and tentacles on the pan and cook for a minute each side — they will curl up.

Arrange the squid on a serving dish. Scatter the roasted pine nuts over the top, dust with paprika and garnish with the chopped parsley. Serve immediately with wedges of lemon to squeeze over the squid and the hummus in a dish.

Prawn skewers with garlicky walnut tarator sauce

One of the most popular ways to enjoy the prawns/shrimp caught off the eastern Mediterranean coast, the Red Sea, the Arabian Sea and the Gulf is to thread them onto skewers with peppers and tomatoes, rather like a shish kebab/kabob. In some of the coastal restaurants, scallops and lobster tails are also prepared this way. Accompanied by lemon or lime wedges to squeeze over them and a hot, tangy sauce or a garlicky, nutty one, this is a delicious way to enjoy the succulent shellfish of the region. The traditional tarator sauce of Turkey is a popular option and can be prepared with walnuts, almonds or pine nuts.

16 large prawns/shrimp

freshly squeezed juice of 2 unwaxed lemons

4 garlic cloves, crushed

1 teaspoon roasted cumin seeds, ground

1 teaspoon smoked paprika

sea salt

8–12 cherry tomatoes

1 green (bell) pepper, cut into bite-size pieces

1 unwaxed lemon, cut into wedges

FOR THE SAUCE

2 slices of white or brown bread with the crusts cut off

freshly squeezed juice of 1–2 unwaxed lemons

120 g/1 cup shelled and toasted walnuts

3 garlic cloves

1 teaspoon ground cumin

3–4 tablespoons olive oil

1 teaspoon finely chopped dried red chilli/chile pepper

1 small bunch fresh coriander/cilantro, finely chopped

sea salt and freshly ground black pepper

charcoal grill/barbecue

8 metal skewers

Serves 4

Shell the prawns/shrimp down to the tail, leaving a little bit of shell at the end. Remove the veins and pop the prawns/shrimp into a shallow dish. Mix together the lemon juice, garlic, cumin, paprika and a little salt and rub it into the prawns/shrimp. Set aside to marinate for 30 minutes.

Meanwhile, prepare the charcoal grill and the sauce. Soak the bread in the lemon juice. Using a pestle and mortar or an electric blender or food processor, pound or grind the walnuts until they resemble sugar crystals. Add the soaked bread, garlic and cumin, pounding the mixture to a paste, then drizzle in the olive oil, beating all the time, until the mixture is thick and creamy. Beat in the chilli/chile and half the coriander/cilantro, season to taste and put aside.

Thread the prawns/shrimp onto metal skewers, alternating with the tomatoes and green (bell) peppers, until all the ingredients are used up. Place the skewers on an oiled rack over the glowing coals and cook them for 2–3 minutes each side, basting with any of the leftover marinade, until the prawns/shrimp are tender and the tomatoes and peppers are lightly browned. Garnish the skewers with the rest of the coriander/cilantro and serve with the walnut tarator sauce.

vegetables, grains and pickles

Lentils with rice and caramelized onions

The medieval Arabic name for this dish of rice and lentils is 'mujaddara', meaning 'smallpox', as the lentils dotted through the rice look like the pockmarks on a face! This unappealing description of a dish you might be about to eat is, however, redeemed in the modern kitchen where it is reputed to be a descendant of the 'mess of pottage' with which Jacob bought Esau's birthright. Called 'megadarra' in Egypt and 'mudardara' in Syria and Jordan, it is regarded as a dish of the poor but, because it is regarded as Esau's favourite, it is a compliment to serve it to guests who in turn thank the hostess for presenting them with this humble dish. Prepared with brown or red lentils and accompanied with dollops of thick, creamy yogurt, it is prepared for Lent in Christian households and Jews eat it as one of their traditional dairy meals on Thursday nights. Topped with caramelized onions and drizzled with melted butter, it can be served on its own or as an accompaniment to grilled and roasted dishes.

3 tablespoons Samna (page 13), or 3 tablespoons olive oil with a knob/pat of butter

3 large onions, halved and finely sliced

2–3 garlic cloves, finely chopped

2 teaspoons cumin seeds

2 teaspoons coriander seeds

1 teaspoon ground fenugreek

1 teaspoon granulated sugar

250 g/1¼ cups brown or red lentils, rinsed and drained

1 litre/1 quart stock or water

250 g/1¼ cups medium or long-grain rice, rinsed and drained

sea salt and freshly ground black pepper

a small bunch of fresh flat-leaf parsley, finely chopped

4–6 generous tablespoons thick, creamy yogurt, to serve

Serves 4–6

Heat the samna, or olive oil and butter in a heavy-based pan and stir in the onions for 5–6 minutes, until they turn golden brown.

Tip half of the onions with most of the samna, or olive oil and butter into a small pan and put it aside. Return the pan to the heat and stir the garlic, spices and sugar into the remaining onions for 1–2 minutes.

Add the lentils, ensuring they are coated in the onions and spices, and pour in the stock or water. Bring the water to the boil, reduce the heat and cook gently for 10 minutes, until the lentils are slightly cooked but al dente. Stir in the rice, bring the liquid back to the boil and season with salt and pepper. Reduce the heat and cook gently for about 10–15 minutes, until all the liquid has been absorbed. Turn off the heat, cover the pot with a clean tea/dish towel, followed by the lid and leave the rice to steam for 10 minutes.

Meanwhile, heat up the remaining onions in a small pan and keep frying them until they turn dark brown and slightly caramelized. Tip the rice and lentils in a mound on a serving dish, scatter the caramelized onions over the top and drizzle with any samna or oil and butter left in the pan. Garnish with parsley and serve immediately with a dollop of yogurt.

Roasted vegetables with yogurt, tahini and pomegranate seeds

Interesting combinations of seasonal vegetables and fruit – roasted, fried or grilled – are common fare on the Middle Eastern mezze table or as an accompaniment to roasted and grilled meat and fish. In some regions this type of dish is called 'shakshuka' and can be varied to include eggs broken into the mix of vegetables towards the end of the cooking time. Served with a garlicky yogurt sauce, this is a delicious way to enjoy vegetables. At home, I like to prepare this dish as a main course and serve it with chunks of crusty bread and a leafy salad.

2 aubergines/eggplants, partially peeled and cut into thin wedges

2 courgettes/zucchini, partially peeled, halved and sliced lengthways or cut into wedges

2 red or yellow (bell) peppers, with stalk and seeds removed and cut into quarters

100–200 ml/½–¾ cup olive oil

8–10 cherry or baby plum tomatoes

2 firm peaches, peeled, stoned and cut into wedges

1 teaspoon roasted fennel seeds

1 teaspoon roasted coriander seeds

500 g/2 cups thick, creamy yogurt

2–3 garlic cloves, crushed

sea salt and freshly ground black pepper

2 tablespoons pine nuts

2 tablespoons tahini, well beaten to the consistency of pouring cream

seeds of half a pomegranate

earthenware or ovenproof dish

Serves 4–6

Preheat the oven to 200°C (400°F) Gas 6.

Place the aubergines/eggplants, courgettes/zucchini and (bell) peppers in an earthenware or ovenproof dish. Drizzle the oil over them and pop them in the preheated oven for 30 minutes, turning them in the oil once or twice. Add the tomatoes, peaches and spices, along with a little extra olive oil if necessary, and return them to the oven for 20 minutes.

In a bowl, beat the yogurt with the garlic and season to taste with salt and pepper. In a small heavy-based pan, dry roast the pine nuts until they give off a nutty aroma and turn golden brown. Tip them into a dish and put aside.

When the roasted vegetables are ready, arrange them on a serving dish. Spoon the yogurt over them, drizzle the tahini in swirls and scatter the roasted pine nuts and pomegranate seeds over the top. Serve while the vegetables are still hot.

Vegetables, fruit and nuts

It wasn't by chance that a big chunk of the eastern Mediterranean was once known as the Fertile Crescent – it has been home to some of the most abundant vegetable, fruit and nut produce in the Middle East. Although much of the harvest, such as courgettes/zucchini, onions, artichokes, figs, pomegranates, dates, pistachios and pine nuts is indigenous to the Middle Eastern region, it didn't reach its full culinary glory until the advent of medieval cookery during the Golden Age of Islam, which was greatly influenced by the court cuisine of Persia. Many dishes were dedicated to vegetables alone, some were combined with fruit in stews, others were stuffed with meat, nuts and rice, or served with a pounded nut sauce, but all were held in such esteem that they became the focus of some Arab sayings, such as 'Vegetables are the ornaments of the dining table' or 'A table without vegetables is like an old man devoid of wisdom'.

Aubergines/eggplants were newcomers to the region and ended up on the banqueting tables of Persia. Originally from India, they travelled the overland trade routes and were adopted by the conquering Arabs who fell under their spell in the 7th and 8th centuries and spread their versatility throughout the Islamic Empire. Aubergines/eggplants play a big role in the culinary culture of Lebanon, Syria and Turkey where they are sometimes known as 'poor man's meat' as they are substantial in content and can act as a substitute for meat in many dishes. Also known as 'the mad apple' the aubergine/eggplant has traditionally been dried in the sun or preserved in salt to be used in the winter, pickled in vinegar with garlic, celery and chillies/chiles, or poached with sugar to make a unique jam. The Turks, who harbour a great love for the aubergine/eggplant, are reputed to feature at least 200 aubergine/eggplant dishes on their national menu.

During the 16th and 17th centuries the Ottomans introduced new vegetables, such as tomatoes, (bell) peppers, pumpkins, potatoes and corn, from the New World as a result of their trade alliance with Spain and spread them throughout their empire, enhancing a regional cuisine that was already well established and versatile. It is almost unthinkable that tomatoes, like chillies/chiles, arrived so late in a region that now incorporates them in so many savoury dishes, you can't imagine how the culinary culture progressed without them. The Seljuks and the Ottomans also spread their art of balancing the warming and cooling properties of food, based on the ancient Chinese principle of Yin and Yang, and this became particularly notable in the vegetable dishes of the region. In Lebanon and Syria, the Christian communities enjoy a number of these well-balanced, easy-to-digest vegetarian dishes when holding the fasts prescribed by the Eastern Orthodox, Catholic and Armenian Churches.

The markets of the Middle East have changed little since medieval times as, except for a few later additions, the same vegetables and fruit are grown and consumed. Depending on the season, the vegetable stalls will offer a healthy-looking range of spinach and beet leaves, carrots, squashes, beans, artichokes, cucumbers, melokhia (Jew's mallow), pumpkins, okra, leeks, courgettes/zucchini, and aubergines/eggplants, all neatly arranged in rows next to the boldly coloured pomegranates, figs, apples, grapes, quinces, apricots, and dates, and flanked by bunches of fresh herbs and crates of preserves and nuts. On the culinary map, vegetables and fruit often go together and nuts, particularly walnuts, almonds, pine nuts, hazelnuts, and pistachios, are never far away as they are used in fillings and sauces for both.

Although seasonal fruit, such as juicy, ripe melons, sweet-smelling peaches, and plump, purple cherries, is mainly eaten fresh, there are several desserts, preserves, and drinks, which feature poached or dried fruits. Apricots, plums and figs are often baked or poached and filled with cream or nuts; sherbet drinks are prepared with fruits like lemons and sour/tart cherries; and puréed fruit is spread on sheets to dry in the sun and form fruit leathers. Unripe fruit and nuts, such as tart green plums, the immature furry green almonds, and tiny green figs are sought-after for pickles and jam.

Fruit and nuts have many stories to tell; Muhammad is reputed to have adored figs and commented that they must be Heaven-sent; the evolution of the traditional fig trees, such as the small Smyrna variety, is one of nature's wonders as the flower has to be visited by a particular tiny wasp in order to bear fruit; in the Middle Ages, Islamic mystics believed pomegranantes could raise the soul and purge it of hate, anger and envy; and then there is the ubiquitous sesame seed which bursts out of its pod when ripe and scatters all over the place, lending credence to the command 'Open sesame' in *Ali Baba and the Forty Thieves*.

Turmeric potatoes with chillies, lime and coriander

Among turmeric's varied uses, as a fabric dye and as an antiseptic, it is renowned for colouring and flavouring food with its a strong yellow colour and earthy, floral taste. Both fresh and dried turmeric are available in the Middle East but the most common is the dried yellow powder, which is often added to meat, grain and potato dishes, such as this popular Arab one, 'battata harra'. You will come across variations of this superb potato dish all over Turkey, Syria, Lebanon, Jordan and the Gulf States, served cold as part of a mezze spread or hot as an accompaniment to almost any grilled or roasted dish. It is extremely easy to prepare and very tasty — thanks to the flavour of turmeric, a fiery kick from the chillies/chiles and a refreshing burst of lime or lemon.

450 g/1 lb. new potatoes

2 tablespoons Samna (page 13), or
2 tablespoons olive oil with a knob/pat
of butter

2—3 garlic cloves, finely chopped

1—2 teaspoons finely chopped dried red
chilli/chile or 1 fresh chilli/chile, seeded
and finely chopped

1—2 teaspoons cumin seeds

1—2 teaspoons coriander seeds

2 teaspoons ground turmeric

freshly squeezed juice of 2 unwaxed limes
or lemons

sea salt and freshly ground black pepper

a bunch of fresh coriander/cilantro, finely
chopped

Serves 4—6

Place the potatoes in a steamer with their skins on and steam for about 10-15 minutes, until cooked but still firm. Drain and refresh under cold running water and peel off the skins. Place the potatoes on a wooden board and cut them into bite-size pieces.

Heat the samna, or olive oil and butter in a heavy-based pan and stir in the garlic, chilli, cumin and coriander seeds for about 2—3 minutes, before adding the turmeric. Toss in the potatoes, coating them in the spices so that they take on the colour of the turmeric. Add the lime juice, making sure it is thoroughly mixed in with the potatoes and spices and, when the pan is almost dry, toss in most of the coriander/cilantro.

Season the dish with salt and pepper and garnish with the rest of the coriander/cilantro. Serve hot as an accompaniment to a main dish, or as a mezze dish, which can be hot or at room temperature.

Fried carrot and fennel with cumin and pomegranate syrup

In the Middle East, vegetable dishes are often served on their own or as part of a mezze spread, but there are some dishes that work well as an accompaniment to roasted or grilled meat and poultry. You can fry or grill any combination of vegetables for this but the aniseed flavour of fennel marries well with root vegetables and fruit. Moroccans employ fennel quite frequently in salads, combined with oranges and apples, and in shellfish and vegetable tagines. In the rest of the Middle East, it is favoured grilled or in salads; or in fusion combinations, such as this delicious recipe.

Heat the samna, or olive oil and butter in a wide, heavy-based pan and fry the carrot and fennel for roughly 2 minutes on each side, until they turn nicely golden in colour. Add the garlic, cumin seeds, fennel seeds and sugar and cook for 1–2 minutes, until slightly caramelized.

Season well and arrange the carrot and fennel on a serving dish. Scatter the preserved lemon over the top, drizzle with the pomegranate syrup/molasses and garnish with the dill and parsley. Serve warm or at room temperature as an accompaniment to grilled or roasted meat and poultry.

3 tablespoons Samna (page 13), or 3 tablespoons olive oil with a knob/pat of butter

2 medium carrots, peeled, halved crossways and cut into long, thin slices

2 small fennel bulbs, trimmed and finely sliced

2 garlic cloves, crushed

2 teaspoons cumin seeds

1 teaspoon fennel seeds

1–2 teaspoons granulated sugar

sea salt and freshly ground black pepper

the rind of half preserved lemon, finely sliced (page 16)

2 tablespoons pomegranate syrup/molasses

a small bunch of fresh dill, finely chopped

a small bunch of fresh flat-leaf parsley, finely chopped

Serves 4

Jewelled Rice

This is a truly sumptuous rice dish, as beautiful to behold as it is to taste. Packed with colourful dried fruit and nuts, which vary according to the region – dates in the variations from Iraq and the United Arab Emirates and orange peel and preserved lemon in Morocco – but the king of all the variations is from Iran as the dish is of Persian origin. Pale yellow with saffron, dotted with barberries which look like rubies amongst the gleaming sultanas/golden raisins, orange apricots and green pistachios, this 'morasa' polow' is glorious and elegant. It is quite rightly reserved for wedding banquets and is sometimes finished off with a flurry of crystallized sugar strands, rose petals or a dusting of icing/confectioners' sugar.

600 ml/2½ cups water

sea salt

a pinch of saffron fronds/threads

450 g/2¼ cups basmati long-grain rice, rinsed and drained

2 tablespoons barberries

2 tablespoons dried sour/tart cherries or cranberries

2 tablespoons currants

2 tablespoons golden sultanas

2 tablespoons raisins

2 tablespoons granulated sugar

2 tablespoons orange blossom water

2 tablespoons freshly squeezed lemon juice

2 tablespoons bitter orange peel, very finely sliced

2 tablespoons Samna (page 13), or 2 tablespoons olive oil with a knob/pat of butter

120 g/1 cup blanched almonds, cut into slivers

120 g/1 cup unsalted pistachio kernels, cut into slivers

2 tablespoons pine nuts

2 tablespoons dried apricots, finely sliced

icing/confectioners' sugar and rose petals, to serve

Serves 6

Pour the water into a pot and bring it to the boil with a pinch of salt. Stir in the saffron fronds/threads and the rice and continue to boil for 3–4 minutes, then reduce the heat and simmer for 10 minutes until the water has been absorbed. Turn off the heat, cover the pot with a clean tea/dish towel, put on the lid and leave the rice to steam a further 10 minutes.

Meanwhile, put the barberries, sour/tart cherries, currants, sultanas and raisins into a bowl. Pour over enough boiling water to cover them, and soak for 5 minutes, then drain and put aside.

In a small pot, stir the sugar with the orange blossom water and lemon juice until the sugar has dissolved. Bring the liquid to the boil, stir in the orange peel and simmer for 5 minutes. Turn off the heat and put aside.

In a wide, heavy-based pan, heat up the samna, or olive oil and butter and stir in the nuts and apricots for 1–2 minutes, until they emit a lovely aroma. Toss in the soaked dried fruit for 1–2 minutes, until they plump up. Tip the rice into the pan and toss it carefully, making sure it is thoroughly mixed with the fruit and nuts. Lift the orange peel out of the syrup and toss most of it through the rice.

Tip the jewelled rice in a mound on a serving dish. Scatter the rest of the orange peel over the top and drizzle the syrup over the rice. Garnish with a dusting of icing/confectioners' sugar and fresh rose petals, and serve immediately on its own or with a simple dish of grilled meat, poultry or vegetables.

Spicy chickpeas and onions with yogurt and pitta bread

A number of popular dishes in Egypt, Lebanon, Jordan and Syria fall into a category called 'fatta', which is an Arabic word denoting the crumbling or breaking of toasted flat bread into small pieces with the hands. All fatta dishes have a base layer of toasted bread soaked in the cooking broth which acts as a bed for the ensuing layered ingredients, such as cubed lamb, spinach or chickpeas, which are then topped with a generous dollop of thick, creamy yogurt. Simple and tasty, fatta dishes are just as common in rural areas as they are in urban ones as they are cooked as street food, family meals and filling snacks for field workers. This dish of chickpeas on toasted pitta bread, fattet hummus, is a great street favourite at any time of day.

250 g/1¼ cups dried chickpeas, soaked overnight

2 fresh bay leaves

3–4 peppercorns

600 ml/2½ cups thick, creamy yogurt

2–3 garlic cloves, crushed

sea salt and freshly ground black pepper

3–4 pitta breads

1 large red onion, cut into bite-size pieces

2–3 tablespoons olive oil

freshly squeezed juice of 1 unwaxed lemon

2 garlic cloves crushed

1–2 teaspoons cumin seeds, roasted and lightly crushed

1–2 teaspoons paprika or finely chopped dried chilli/chile

1–2 teaspoons dried mint

2 tablespoons pine nuts

2 tablespoons Samna (page 13), or 2 tablespoons olive oil with a knob/pat of butter

Serves 4

Drain the chickpeas and tip them into a pot. Cover with plenty of water and bring it to the boil. Add the bay leaves and peppercorns, reduce the heat and simmer for 1 hour, until tender.

Meanwhile, beat the yogurt with the garlic in a bowl and season it with salt and pepper. Toast the pitta breads, break them up into bite-size pieces and arrange them on a serving dish or bowl.

Drain the chickpeas and reserve roughly 4 tablespoons of the cooking liquid. While still hot, tip the chickpeas into a bowl and add the onion, olive oil, lemon juice, garlic, cumin, paprika and most of the dried mint.

Moisten the pitta breads with the reserved cooking liquid and spread the chickpeas over them. Spoon the yogurt over the top and sprinkle with the reserved dried mint.

Roast the pine nuts in a frying pan/skillet until they turn golden brown and emit a nutty aroma. Add the samna, or olive oil and butter and, as soon as it melts, pour the mixture over the yogurt. Serve immediately, while the chickpeas are still warm.

Baked stuffed dumplings with yogurt

This ancient baked dumpling dish, 'mantı', falls somewhere between a Chinese dumpling and Italian pasta. Traditionally, the noodle dough is stuffed, baked in the oven and served with garlic-flavoured yogurt and drizzled with melted butter. The more modern version, favoured by Istanbul socialites, involves boiling the stuffed pasta parcels and serving them with plain yogurt and a tomato sauce. Variations of these dumplings are popular in Turkey and in the eastern Mediterranean – in Lebanon and Syria, they are called 'shish barak' – some are stuffed with minced/ground lamb or beef, while others are filled with mashed chickpeas or chopped nuts.

FOR THE DOUGH

450 g/3 lbs plain/all-purpose flour

½ teaspoon salt

1 egg and 1 yolk, beaten

roughly 50 ml/¼ cup water

FOR THE FILLING

a 400-g/14.5 oz. can of chickpeas, rinsed and drained

1–2 teaspoons cumin seeds, roasted and ground

1–2 teaspoons dried red chilli/chile, finely chopped

sea salt

FOR THE YOGURT

500 g/2 cups thick, creamy yogurt

2–3 garlic cloves, crushed

sea salt and freshly ground black pepper

TO SERVE

600 ml/2½ cups vegetable or chicken stock

2 tablespoons Samna (page 13), or olive oil with a knob/pat of butter

1 teaspoon dried chilli/chile or paprika, finely chopped

1 small bunch fresh flat-leaf parsley, finely chopped, to serve

ovenproof dish

Serves 4–6

Preheat the oven to 200°C (400°F) Gas 6.

First make the dough. Sift the flour with the salt into a wide bowl. Make a well in the centre and pour in the beaten egg. Add the water and, using your finger, draw in the flour to form a dough. Knead the dough for about 10 minutes, then cover the bowl with a clean, damp tea/dish towel, and leave it to rest for about 1 hour.

Meanwhile, prepare the filling and the yogurt sauce. In a bowl, mash the chickpeas with a fork. Beat in the cumin and chopped chilli/chile, season with salt and pepper and put aside. In another bowl, beat the yogurt with the garlic, season it to your taste and put aside.

Roll out the noodle dough as thinly as possible on a lightly floured surface. Using a sharp knife, cut the dough into small squares (roughly 2.5 cm/1 in. squares). Spoon a little of the chickpea mixture into the middle of each square and bunch the corners together to form a little pouch that is almost sealed at the top. Place the filled pasta parcels in a greased ovenproof dish, stacking them next to each other so they don't fall over, and bake them in the preheated oven, uncovered, for 15–20 minutes, until the tops turn golden-brown.

Pour the stock into a pan and bring it to the boil. Take the golden pasta parcels out of the oven and pour the stock over them – there should be enough to just cover the parcels and no more. Return the dish to the oven and bake for a further 15–20 minutes, until almost all the stock has been absorbed.

Transfer the freshly baked dumplings to a serving dish and spoon the yogurt sauce over them. Quickly melt the samna, or olive oil and butter with the chopped chilli/chile and pour it over the top. Garnish with a little parsley and serve immediately while the dumplings are still hot.

Couscous with seven vegetables

This is a classic Moroccan couscous dish, which is enjoyed throughout North Africa. The number seven is believed to bring good luck so, as long as you have that number of vegetables in the accompanying stew, you can be flexible with the variety. When couscous dishes like this one are cooked in the Middle East, they are often referred to as 'Maghrebia', meaning a dish from the Maghreb – Morocco, Tunisia and Algeria – as couscous is one of those ingredients that has travelled with the invading and colonizing Arabs. With the influence of the French in Morocco and in Lebanon, you find couscous dishes are more common in the eastern Mediterranean than any other part of the Middle East. If you have a couscoussier (a traditional two-chambered steamer made of either ceramic or metal), you can steam the couscous in the compartment above the vegetables cooking in the stock in the lower part, or simply follow this recipe.

FOR THE COUSCOUS
500 g/2½ cups medium couscous

600 ml/2½ cups warm water

1 teaspoon salt

2 tablespoons sunflower oil

roughly 25 g/2 tablespoons butter, cut into small pieces

FOR THE VEGETABLE STEW
1 tablespoon Harissa (page 14)

6 garlic cloves, peeled and smashed

a few sprigs of rosemary

2 fresh bay leaves

6–8 peppercorns

1 teaspoon sea salt

a bunch of fresh flat-leaf parsley

a bunch of fresh coriander/cilantro

4 medium carrots, peeled, halved and cut in half lengthways

2 medium sweet potatoes, peeled, halved lengthways and cut into long, thick strips

2 onions, peeled and cut into quarters

2 celery stalks, trimmed and cut into 3 pieces

2 leeks, trimmed and cut into 3–4 pieces

1 small marrow or 2 courgettes/ zucchini, halved and cut into long, thick strips

2–3 tomatoes, cut into quarters

2 teaspoons honey

a small bunch of fresh coriander/cilantro, finely chopped, to serve

ovenproof dish

dampened parchment paper

Serves 6

Preheat the oven to 180°C (350°F) Gas 4.

Put the couscous into an ovenproof dish and pour in the water combined with the salt. Stir once to make sure all the grains are submerged, cover with a damp tea/dish towel and leave to plump up for 10 minutes.

Rake a fork through the couscous to loosen the grains then, using your fingers, rub the oil into them, lifting the grains up into the air and letting them fall back into the dish to air them. Dot the top of the couscous with the butter, cover with the parchment paper and pop it into the preheated oven for 15 minutes.

Meanwhile, fill a pot with 1.8 litres/2 quarts water and bring it to the boil. Stir in the harissa, garlic, rosemary, bay leaves, peppercorns and salt. Add the herbs, carrots and sweet potatoes and cook for 5 minutes. Next add the onions, celery, leeks and marrow. Put the lid on the pot and cook gently for 5 minutes, until all the vegetables are tender. Check the seasoning of the stock and stir in the tomatoes and honey.

Pile the couscous in a mound on a shallow serving dish. Using a slotted spoon, lift the vegetables out of the stock and place some of the long strips against the sides of the couscous mound and the rest around the base. Garnish the dish with the coriander/cilantro, then quickly strain the stock into a bowl and serve it alongside the couscous and vegetables.

Baked quinces stuffed with aromatic rice

Medieval, Mevlevi and Ottoman recipes call for an assortment of vegetables and fruit to be stuffed and cooked in lemon juice, grape or pomegranate syrup/molasses, or in olive oil. The most common of these include (bell) peppers, courgettes/zucchini, tomatoes, plums, apricots, apples, and the most exquisite of all, quinces. The 'golden apple' given by Paris to Aphrodite is thought to be a quince and the Romans referred to them as 'honey apples'. When cooked in sugar, the pale flesh turns a beautiful shade of pink and emits a heavenly floral scent that fills the kitchen and, when baked or roasted, they emerge fragrant from the oven. The most common fillings for quinces or any other fruit and vegetable are aromatic rice, or minced/ground lamb and minced/ground beef. You can follow this recipe using apples or quinces but the latter require a bit of time to cook before you can hollow them out to stuff.

4 large quinces, washed and well rubbed

2 tablespoons Samna (page 13), or 2 tablespoons olive oil with a knob/pat of butter

1 onion, finely chopped

2 garlic cloves

2 tablespoons pine nuts

2 tablespoons currants, soaked in warm water for 5 minutes and drained

1–2 teaspoons ground cinnamon

1–2 teaspoons ground allspice

1 teaspoon sugar

175 g/1 scant cup short-grain rice, rinsed and drained

salt and freshly ground black pepper

a bunch of fresh flat-leaf parsley, finely chopped, plus extra to garnish

a bunch of fresh dill fronds, finely chopped

2–3 vine tomatoes, finely sliced

FOR THE COOKING LIQUID

2 tablespoons olive oil

freshly squeezed juice of 1 unwaxed lemon

1–2 teaspoons granulated sugar

baking sheet, lined with foil

ovenproof dish

Serves 4

Preheat the oven to 170°C (325°F) Gas 3.

Place the quinces on the lined baking sheet. Roast them in the preheated oven for about 1½ hours, until they feel soft to the touch. Leave them to rest until they're cool enough to handle.

Heat the samna, or olive oil and butter in a heavy based pan. Fry the onion and garlic, until they soften. Add the pine nuts and currants, and fry until the pine nuts turn golden, then stir in the spices and sugar. Toss in the rice, making sure it is well mixed, and pour in enough water to cover the rice (roughly 1–2 cm/½ in. above the grains). Bring it to the boil. Season with salt and pepper, give it a stir, then reduce the heat and leave it to simmer until almost all the water has been absorbed. Add the herbs and turn off the heat. Cover the pan with a dry tea/dish towel, followed by the lid, and leave the rice to steam for 5 minutes.

Meanwhile, prepare the quinces. Cut them open lengthways and remove the cores with a small knife. Scoop out a bit of the flesh to create a deep enough hollow for the filling, chop the flesh finely and stir it through the rice. Spoon the rice into the quince hollows and place them in an ovenproof dish.

In a small bowl, mix together the olive oil, lemon juice and sugar with 2–3 tablespoons water, stirring until the sugar dissolves. Arrange 2 slices of tomato over the rice filling in each quince half and pour over the oil and lemon juice mixture.

Turn up the oven to 180°C (350°F) Gas 4 and put in the quinces to bake for about 25 minutes, basting them with the olive oil and lemon mixture once or twice. Garnish the baked quinces with a little parsley and serve on their own with a salad or as an accompaniment to grilled or roasted meats.

Preserves

Pickling and preserving is a particularly important method of food preservation in the Middle East, partly because it ensures the harvest is not wasted and can easily be distributed but also because the combinations of fruit, vegetables and nuts can be spectacularly savoury and the pickling liquid is deliciously thirst-quenching on a hot day. Only the freshest or unripe fruit and vegetables are employed in pickles so that they retain the desired bite to them and the liquid generally consists of grape or apple vinegar mixed with water and salt or just brine. Almost every conceivable vegetable and unripe fruit is pickled, such as tiny cucumbers, white cabbage, green chillies/chiles, okra, green tomatoes, whole peeled garlic cloves, green plums, lemons, limes, carrots, grapes, green almonds in their furry skins and unripe apricots. Pickle shops and stalls also display the much sought-after traditional combinations such as little white turnips combined with slices of beetroot to turn the flesh a pretty shade of purple, 'torshi left' — similarly cauliflower florets are combined with red cabbage to turn them pink — and baby aubergines/eggplants stuffed with walnuts, 'batinjan makdous'.

Pickled purple turnips

8 small white turnips

4 garlic cloves, peeled

1 small raw beet(root), or 2 slices large beet(root)

300 ml/1¼ cups white wine vinegar or cider vinegar

300ml/1¼ cups water

1 teaspoon sea salt

sterilized jar with vinegar-proof lid

Trim and peel the turnips. Rinse then pat dry and pop them into a sterilized jar with the garlic. Trim and peel the beet(root), cut into 2–3 slices and add them to the jar. Mix together the vinegar and water with the salt and pour the liquid over the turnips and beet(root). Seal the jar with a vinegar-proof lid and store for 1–2 weeks, until the turnips have taken on a purplish-pink hue.

Pickled stuffed aubergines

12 baby aubergines/eggplants, round or oblong, with stalks removed

1 leek, trimmed and cut in half if very long

225 g / 1½ cups walnuts, finely chopped

1 red (bell) pepper, seeded and finely chopped

4 garlic cloves, finely chopped

1 fresh red or green chilli/chile, seeded and finely chopped

1–2 teaspoons sea salt

1 tablespoon olive oil

a small bunch of fresh flat-leaf parsley

600 ml/2½ cups white wine vinegar

sterilized jars with vinegar-proof lids

Serves 4–6

Bring a pot of water to the boil and drop in the aubergines/eggplants and the leek for about 10 minutes to soften. Drain and refresh under cold running water. Leave the aubergines/eggplants to drain in a colander while you prepare the filling. Cut the leek into long thin strips and put aside.

In a bowl, mix together the walnuts, (bell) pepper, garlic and fresh chilli/chile. Add the salt and bind with the olive oil. Using a sharp knife, make a slit in the side of each aubergine/eggplant, like a pouch, and stuff the hollow with the filling. Finish with a few parsley leaves stuffed in at the end and carefully wind a strip of leek around the aubergine/eggplant to bind it and keep it intact.

Place the bound aubergines/eggplants in a bowl or sterilized jars, packed in tightly, and pour over the vinegar – you can combine the vinegar with oil if you prefer. Cover the bowl with clingfilm/plastic wrap or seal the jars, and store in a cool place for 2–3 weeks. As long as they are always sealed and topped up with vinegar, these aubergines/eggplants will keep for several months.

Carrot, almond and cardamom conserve

'Heavenly' and 'scented', 'exotic' and 'delicate' are words to describe the myriad of jams and sweet preserves in the Middle East. Some conjure up images of ancient civilizations, others of medieval banquets, but almost all have one thing in common — they are prepared in the fashion of a syrupy conserve so that they can be spooned, rather than spread, onto bread, pancakes, yogurt, clotted cream, baked fruit, milk puddings, cakes and sweetmeats. Some are so special they are presented in crystal bowls and served with silver spoons; others are more rustic and can appear at every meal to stir into tea or to eat with lumps of salty cheese. Quince, green fig, rose petal, coconut, date, strawberry, dried fig, plum tomato, sour/tart cherry, mulberry, watermelon, aubergine/eggplant, clementine and apricot are just some of the many traditional conserves of the region. And there is this delicious carrot and almond one, which is often flavoured with cardamom in Iran, with mastic and orange blossom water in Turkey and with cloves in other parts of the Middle East.

2 oranges

425 ml/1¾ cups water

700 g/3 cups granulated sugar

seeds of 5-6 cardamom pods

900 g/2 lbs. carrots, peeled and sliced into very fine rounds

2–3 tablespoons blanched almonds, cut into slivers

2 tablespoons rose water

freshly squeezed juice of 1 unwaxed lemon

sterilized jar (optional)

Serves 6–8

Cut the oranges in half and squeeze them to extract the juice. Using a small sharp knife, cut the peel off and trim away any pith. Slice the peel very finely.

Pour the water into a heavy-based saucepan, add the orange juice and the sugar and bring it to the boil, stirring all the time. Stir in the cardamom seeds and keep the liquid boiling for 2–3 minutes, then reduce the heat and simmer gently for 5–10 minutes until it has thickened a little and is quite syrupy.

Add the carrots, almond slivers and the finely sliced orange peel and bring the syrup back to the boil, stirring all the time. Reduce the heat and simmer for 10–15 minutes. Stir in the rose water and lemon juice and simmer for another 5 minutes.

Turn off the heat and leave the conserve to cool in the saucepan. Spoon it into a bowl and serve it with rice pudding, yogurt, vanilla ice cream or warm scones, pancakes and bread. Alternatively, spoon the conserve into sterilized jars and store them in a cool place for 2–3 months to enjoy as a special treat.

sweet dishes and drinks

Quinces poached in clove syrup with buffalo cream

3 quinces (about 3½ lbs./1.5 kg)

freshly squeezed juice of 1 unwaxed lemon

300 ml/1¼ cups water

200 ml/1 cup granulated sugar

6 whole cloves

6 generous tablespoons chilled clotted buffalo cream, ordinary clotted cream, crème fraîche or Labna (prepared overnight, page 18)

Serves 6

In Turkey this dessert is flavoured with cloves, in Iran it is flavoured with cardamom and in other parts of the Middle East a spice is not always included but, whichever way you prepare the quinces, the result is quite magical. Clotted cream that is so thick it can be cut with a knife or rolled into a log, called 'kaymak' in Turkish and 'eishta' in Arabic, is prepared from the rich milk of water buffalo and is served as the traditional accompaniment to this and many other desserts but you can substitute it with ordinary clotted cream, crème fraîche or 'labna', the homemade yogurt cheese (page 18). Related to the pear and the apple, a quince looks rather like a large, slightly misshapen, yellow apple. In its raw form it is quite difficult to eat as the fruit makes your tongue feel like it is sticking to the roof of your mouth, so it is usually cooked in both savoury and sweet dishes. The wonderful thing about poaching quinces in syrup is that the yellow fruit transforms into a pretty shade of pink, the pectin in the fruit and the seeds turn the syrup into a jelly on cooling and the aroma emitted from the poaching fruit is simply heavenly – that alone is reason enough to make this dessert!

Peel the quinces, halve them lengthways and remove the core and seeds with a sharp knife, leaving a shallow hollow in the centre of each half. Keep the seeds.

Fill a large bowl with cold water, stir in half of the lemon juice and submerge the quince halves in it to prevent them from discolouring.

Pour the water into a heavy-based pan and stir in the sugar and the rest of the lemon juice. Bring the liquid to the boil, stirring all the time until the sugar has dissolved. Add the quince seeds and the cloves to the pan and boil the liquid gently for 2–3 minutes, until it begins to resemble a thin syrup.

Slip the quince halves into the syrup, bring the syrup back to the boil, then reduce the heat and poach the fruit gently, basting from time to time, for about 50 minutes, until they are tender and have turned pink. Turn off the heat and leave the quinces to cool in the pan and the syrup to turn to jelly.

Pick the seeds out of the jelly and transfer the quince to a serving dish, spooning the jelly around them. You can retain or discard the cloves – that's up to you. Serve the quince chilled or at room temperature with a spoonful of clotted buffalo cream or crème fraîche in the hollow in the middle of each half.

Fresh figs with yogurt cheese and rose petal jam

The Prophet Muhammad was reputed to have described the fig as a fruit from paradise and it is also often referred to in the Bible. Rose petals have also been held in high esteem – the ancient Egyptians bathed in them and the Romans and Persians scented their water and wine with them – so the combination of the exquisite and delicately scented rose petal jam with one of the most exotic and ancient fruits of the Middle East could be regarded as paradise on a plate! Add a dollop of something chilled and creamy – labna (or yogurt cheese), clotted cream, ice cream or crème fraîche – and you have a pudding of sheer exotic indulgence. There are several varieties of fig in the Middle East, particularly in Turkey and North Africa, but the purple figs are the most common and when they are ripened on the tree they have a sticky, honey-flavoured, pinky-orange interior.

450 g/1 lb. fresh, scented, pink or red rose petals, rinsed and drained

500 ml/2 cups water

1–2 tablespoons rose water (if needed)

450 g/2¼ cups granulated sugar

freshly squeezed juice of 1 unwaxed lemon

12 ripe figs, washed and patted dry

2–3 cinnamon sticks

18 fresh rose petals, for garnishing

Labna (page 18), clotted cream, ice cream or crème fraîche, to serve

Serves 6

Firstly, if you want to serve this dish with labna, you'll need to follow the recipe for straining yogurt overnight (page 18). Preheat the oven to 180°C (350°F) Gas 4.

If necessary, trim and clean the rose petals but, if rinsing, make sure they are thoroughly drained and dried.

Pour the water into a heavy-based pan and bring it to the boil. Stir in the rose petals, reduce the heat and simmer the petals gently for 3–5 minutes, until tender. Strain the petals into a bowl and return the rose-scented water to the pan – if the rose petals don't have a strong scent at this point, then add 1–2 tablespoons rose water at this stage. Put the strained petals aside.

Add the sugar to the rose-scented water and bring it to the boil, stirring all the time. Reduce the heat and simmer for 10 minutes, until the liquid thickens and coats the back of the wooden spoon. Stir in the lemon juice and the strained rose petals and simmer for a further 10 minutes. Leave the mixture to cool in the pan.

Meanwhile, using a sharp knife, cut a deep cross from the top of each fig towards the bottom, keeping the skin at the bottom intact. Fan each fig out a little, so it looks like a flower and place them in a lightly buttered baking dish. Tuck the cinnamon sticks around the figs and drizzle a little of the rose petal jam over each one. Pop the figs into the preheated oven for 15–20 minutes to soften and slightly caramelize. Place the baked figs on a serving dish and spoon a little labna or other chosen filling into each one. Drizzle more of the rose petal jam over them and then sprinkle the fresh rose petals over the top.

Medieval milk pudding with mastic

Chilled and silky, this traditional milk pudding, 'muhallabia', is a classic throughout North Africa, Turkey and the Middle East, as the recipe travelled with the invading Arabs across the region. According to Islamic custom, milk should have ceased flowing before it is consumed so it is generally used to make butter, cheese and yogurt, as well as a variety of milk puddings, which can be as plain or as grand as you desire depending on how you serve them. Traditionally, muhallabia (derived from the Arabic word for milk, 'halib') is flavoured with rose water or orange blossom water, or simply with mastic, the aromatic gum of a tree from the pistachio family, which gives the pudding a unique resinous taste with a slight chewy twang. Mastic also cleanses the palate and will transport you back to summer holidays in Greece or Turkey.

60 g/½ cup rice flour

1 litre/1 quart whole milk

4—6 mastic crystals

150 g/¾ cup granulated sugar

1—2 tablespoons icing/confectioners' sugar (optional)

Serves 6

In a small bowl, combine the rice flour with 4—6 tablespoons of the milk to form a loose paste and put aside. Using a small pestle and mortar, pulverize the mastic crystals with 1—2 teaspoons of the sugar, until it resembles fine sugar crystals, and put aside.

Pour the rest of the milk into a heavy-based saucepan and stir in the sugar. Bring the milk to boiling point, stirring all the time until the sugar has dissolved. Reduce the heat and stir a spoonful or two of the hot milk into the rice flour paste, then tip this paste into the pan, stirring all the time to prevent any lumps forming. Bring the milk back to boiling point and beat in the pulverized mastic with a balloon whisk to break up any lumps of mastic.

Reduce the heat to low and simmer gently for about 15—20 minutes, stirring or beating from time to time, until the mixture becomes thick and coats the back of the spoon.

Pour the mixture into a serving bowl or individual bowls and leave to cool, allowing a skin to form on top. Chill the pudding in the refrigerator and, just before serving, dust the tops with a little icing/confectioners' sugar, if desired.

The Traditions of Coffee

Surrounded by tradition and ritual, coffee is the king of drinks in the Middle East. The plant is thought to have originated in Ethiopia and made its way to Egypt and Arabia where its discovery was interwoven with myths of dancing goats and monks slipping into slumber as the fruity pulp would have been fermented to make a basic wine. The practice of actually roasting the beans to make a hot drink didn't begin until the thirteenth century and, according to legend, coffee was consumed in vast quantities by the Sufis of Yemen as they believed it enhanced their mystical raptures and performances of spiritual whirling.

These whirling dervishes, along with Muslim pilgrims, contributed to the spread of coffee throughout the Middle East and, by the end of the fifteenth century, cultivation of the plant, coffea Arabica, began in Yemen. It is thought that because of the stimulant qualities of the coffee bean, the drink was called 'qahwah' ('kahwa'), a poetic name for wine, and this name has remained to this day. In the sixteenth century, the Ottoman Turks refined the art of coffee-making and spread their version — now known as Turkish coffee - throughout the empire.

In the Middle East today, coffee is a prestigious drink as well as a social one. It is more expensive than tea so, for those who can afford it, the first coffee of the day is enjoyed on rising, the second cup is drunk mid-morning, and a third may be drunk after a long midday meal but, amongst poorer the communities, it is often restricted to ceremonial occasions. In Arab communities, coffee is a social drink for men who often gather in coffee houses to chat and pass the time of day - the Bedouin of Jordan are reputed to consume so much coffee they would collapse without it. In traditional settings throughout the Middle Eastern region, a person of high rank will be served first and men are always served before women. And, in rural Turkey, there still exists the tradition of selecting a suitable bride based on a young girl's ability to prepare and serve coffee, while the prospective mother-in-law and her son inspect her beauty and grace.

The serving and drinking of coffee are steeped in tradition throughout the Middle East and it is often served in small decorative cups on an elaborate brass or silver tray. In general the offering of coffee or tea is regarded as a cultural mark of hospitality but, for some richer individuals, the whole ceremony of serving and drinking can turn into an extravagant display of wealth as the coffee might be poured into tiny cups made of real gold, embedded with precious gems, stirred with ornate silver coffee spoons. In Arab communities, the coffee is often made in two pots — the ground beans are brewed in the first and poured into the second — and cardamom seeds or cinnamon sticks can be added to the brew. For the Turkish version, the beans are ground to a very fine powder, which is brewed in a small pot with a long handle and the coffee is served with a layer of froth. Both types of coffee can be sweetened while brewing or served with sugar, which sometimes involves holding a sugar cube between the teeth and sipping the coffee through it, and milk is never added.

THE RITUALS OF TURKISH COFFEE

To make traditional Turkish coffee, measure the water by the coffee cup (a standard, small cylindrical cup) and the coffee by the teaspoon. The general rule allows for one coffee cup of water to one teaspoon of coffee and one teaspoon of sugar per person. Tip the water into a small pot with a long handle ('cezve') and spoon the coffee and sugar on the top. Use a teaspoon to quickly stir the sugar and coffee into the surface of the water to give the desired froth a kick-start. Put the pan over a medium heat and, using the teaspoon, gradually scrape the outer edges of the surface into the middle to create an island of froth. The key to the creation of a good froth is to always work at the surface, never touch the bottom of the pot with a spoon. Once the coffee is hot, pour about a third of it into the coffee cup to warm it up and return the pan to the heat. Continue to gather the froth in the middle and, just as the coffee begins to bubble up, take it off the heat and pour it into the cup. Leave the coffee cup to stand for a minute to let the coffee grains settle and then drink it while it is hot.

The final ritual in the drinking of traditional Turkish coffee is the reading of one's fortune from the grains. It is customary to turn the coffee cup upside down on the saucer to let the sediment dribble down the inside. Once the cup has cooled, it is turned over and the pattern of rivulets down the sides as well as the sediment in the saucer will determine one's fortune.

Stuffed fresh dates in clementine syrup

Regarded as a gift from God, dates are one of the most ancient staple foods of the region and, as they provide a natural source of minerals and have a high sugar content, they are coveted for their nutritional value as well as their sweetness. It is said that the Bedouin cannot manage to sleep under the fruit-laden date palms, such is their urge to pick the fruit and devour it. As the date has traditionally been integral to the lives of both the nomadic and settled Arabs, it is one of the most extensively cultivated crops, particularly in Iraq, Egypt, Iran and the Arabian Gulf, where there are reputed to be over 350 varieties. Delicious fresh or dried, they are eaten as a sweet snack throughout the Middle East, offered to guests with milk in Morocco and added to many grain dishes, stews and sweetmeats, as well as preserves and puddings. This unusual Arab dessert is normally prepared when red dates are in season but you can use other fresh dates as an alternative.

40 fresh red or yellow dates

40 blanched almonds

500 g/2½ cups granulated sugar

freshly squeezed juice of 2 clementines and the pared rind cut into thick strips

3—4 cloves

thick clotted cream or Labna (page 18) prepared overnight, to serve

sterilized jars (optional)

Serves 6—8

Place the dates in a heavy-based pan and cover with just enough water. Bring the water to the boil, reduce the heat and simmer for 5 minutes to soften the dates. Drain the dates and reserve the water.

Carefully push the stones/pits out of each date with a sharp knife. Stuff each date with an almond and put aside. Pour the reserved date water back into the pan and add the sugar, clementine juice and rind, along with the cloves. Bring the water to the boil, stirring all the time until the sugar has dissolved and continue to boil for 2—3 minutes. Reduce the heat and simmer until the syrup begins to thicken. Pop the dates into the syrup and simmer for about 40 minutes, until the syrup is thick and fragrant.

Leave the dates to cool in the syrup then transfer them to a bowl and serve them chilled or at room temperature, with thick clotted cream, labna, fresh leavened bread, milk puddings or on their own as a sweet treat.

To preserve them, spoon the dates into sterilized jars, cover with the syrup, seal and store in the refrigerator or a cool place for 2—3 months.

Dried fruit and nut compote with orange blossom water

Served as a winter dessert or at ceremonial feasts, this classic fruit compote, 'khoshaf', is a great favourite throughout the whole region. It is also served for breakfast and as a sweet snack at any time of day. When the Ottomans dined in the Topkapı Palace in Istanbul, the compote (called 'hoşaf' in Turkish, derived from the Persian word for 'pleasant water') was often spooned over plain rice as a final touch to a rather splendid meal. Every religious or regional community across the Middle East and North Africa has its own combination of fruit and nuts and the syrup can be flavoured with rose water, orange blossom water or with lemon juice.

225 g/1¾ cups dried apricots

175 g/1⅓ cups dried prunes

120 g/1 cup sultanas/golden raisins

120 g/1 cup blanched almonds

2 tablespoons pine nuts

3–4 tablespoons granulated sugar

3–4 tablespoons orange blossom water

cream, ice cream or rice pudding, to serve

Serves 6

Put the dried fruit and nuts into a large bowl and cover completely with water. Add the sugar and orange blossom water, and gently stir the water until the sugar has dissolved.

Cover the bowl and place it in the refrigerator. Leave the fruit and nuts to soak for 48 hours, during which time the liquid will turn syrupy and golden. Serve chilled either on its own, with cream, ice cream or rice pudding.

Cheese-filled shredded pastry in lemon syrup

This delectable sweet pastry, 'konafa' ('künefe' or 'kadayif' in Turkish) is made with the thin strands of pastry that many visitors to Turkey and the Middle East refer to as shredded wheat. It is one of the most popular sweet dishes in Jordan, particularly amongst the Palestinian community, as well as in Lebanon, Syria and the southern region of Turkey and is often prepared for parties and happy reunions. It is difficult to make at home, since the batter requires pushing through a sieve/strainer onto a hot metal sheet over an open fire but you can buy the ready-prepared pastry, 'kadaif' (also the name given to many pastries made with it), in Middle Eastern, Turkish and Greek food stores. It's sold in packs and looks like pale strands of vermicelli and you can buy individual non-stick pans specially for making 'konafa'. The same pastry is used to make the Turkish sweet 'kız memesi kadayıf', a great favourite of the Ottoman Palace kitchens, and a variety of Middle Eastern syrupy pastry filled with nuts. In Turkey, the cheese most commonly used for the filling of this pastry is the elastic 'dil peyniri', which peels off in threads, but mozzarella is similar in texture and taste, and you can also use ricotta or a cream filling thickened with rice flour.

FOR THE SYRUP

225 g/1 generous cup granulated sugar

125 ml/½ cup water

freshly squeezed juice of 1 unwaxed lemon

FOR THE PASTRY

5 g/7.5 oz. ready-prepared kadaif (shredded pastry)

120 g/½ cup Samna (page 13), melted

350 g/12 oz. dil peyniri or mozzarella cheese, thinly sliced

1–2 tablespoons pistachio kernels, coarsely chopped

shallow baking pan

Serves 4–6

Preheat the oven to 180°C (350°F) Gas 4.

Put the sugar and water into a pan and bring it to the boil, stirring until the sugar has dissolved. Add the lemon juice, reduce the heat and leave the syrup to simmer and thicken for about 15 minutes, until it coats the back of a wooden spoon. Turn off the heat and leave the syrup to cool. Chill it in the refrigerator if you like.

Put the kadaif into a bowl and separate the strands. Pour the melted samna over them and, using your fingers, rub it all over the strands so they are coated in it. Spread half the pastry in the base of a shallow baking pan (the Turks use a round pan roughly 27 cm/11 in. in diameter) and press it down with your fingers. Lay the slices of cheese over the top and cover with the rest of the pastry, pressing it down firmly and tucking it down the sides.

Cook the pastry in the preheated oven for about 45 minutes, until it is golden-brown. Loosen the edges of the pastry with a sharp knife and pour the cold syrup over it — the hot pastry will absorb most of the syrup but you can pop it back into the oven for 2–3 minutes to ensure it does. Scatter the pistachios over the top. Divide the pastry into squares or segments, depending on the shape of your baking pan, and serve while still warm so that the cheese remains melted and soft.

Semolina helva with pine nuts

In contrast to baklava and its associations with happy events, 'helwah' ('helva' in Turkish) is more often linked to religious ceremonies and mourning when it is offered to friends and the poor. However, helwah (meaning 'sweet' in Arabic) is not just restricted to worship and bereavement as it also signifies good fortune and is customarily prepared when moving house or taking on a new job. It is also one of many sweet dishes prepared for the 'Sweet Festival' to mark the end of Ramadan, the Muslim month of fasting. In pre-Islamic Persia, a similar sweet dish called 'sen' was prepared on the last day of the New Year festival to keep up the energy levels of the ancestors on their journey back to heaven after their annual visit to earth. In Iran today, this tradition has faded in most parts of the country although a modern version, halva, is now prepared to mark the death of a loved one and, like Turkey and the rest of the Middle East, it is offered to mourners. This recipe is for the traditional Turkish 'irmik helvasi' but there are several variations combining different nuts and grains, as well as dried fruit.

225 g/2 sticks salted butter

450 g/3 cups ground semolina (flour)

3 tablespoons pine nuts

850 ml/3½ cups whole milk

225 g/1 cup plus 2 tablespoons granulated sugar

1–2 teaspoons ground cinnamon

Serves 6–8

Melt the butter in a heavy-based pan. Stir in the semolina and pine nuts. Cook until lightly browned, stirring all the time.

Reduce the heat and pour in the milk. Mix well, cover the pan with a clean tea/dish towel and press the lid down tightly. Pull up the flaps of the towel over the lid and simmer gently, until the milk has been absorbed.

Add the sugar, stirring until it has dissolved. Cover the pan again with the tea/dish towel and lid and remove from the heat. Leave to stand for 30 minutes, stirring occasionally with a wooden spoon, until the grains are separated. Serve the helva warm or at room temperature, by spooning them into individual bowls and dusting the tops with a little cinnamon.

Noah's pudding

120 g/1 cup whole barley pearls/pearled barley, husks removed, soaked for 24 hours in plenty of cold water

60 g/½ cup haricot/dried white beans, soaked for at least 6 hours or overnight and cooked until tender

60 g/½ cup skinned dried broad/fava beans, soaked for at least 6 hours or overnight and cooked until tender

60 g/½ cup dried chickpeas, soaked for at least 6 hours or overnight and cooked until tender

60 g/⅓ cup short-grain rice, washed and drained

120 g/1 cup dried apricots

60 g/½ cup sultanas/golden raisins

60 g/½ cup raisins

60 g/½ cup (Zante) currants

225 g/1 generous cup granulated sugar

2 tablespoons cornflour/corn starch or rice flour, mixed with a little water to form a creamy paste

150 ml/⅔ cup rose water

TO GARNISH

4–5 dried figs, sliced

4–5 ready-to-eat dried apricots, sliced

1 tablespoon sultanas/golden raisins, soaked in warm water for 10 minutes and drained

1 tablespoon pine nuts

seeds of half a fresh pomegranate

1–2 tablespoons desiccated coconut

Serves 10–12

Called 'Ahsure' in Arabic ('Aşure' in Turkish), this pudding of grains, pulses/dried beans and dried fruit is referred to as 'Noah's pudding' because, according to legend, he made it on the Ark by combining whatever stores were left when the flood subsided. It was also regarded as a sacred pudding by the early Arabs in pre-Islamic times and later became the traditional pudding to serve on the tenth day of Muharam, the first day of the Muslim calendar, to mark the martyrdom of the Prophet's grandson, Imam Huseyin. It is a pudding that requires a fair amount of advance preparation and is always made in large quantities to be shared with friends.

Tip the barley and its soaking water into a large, deep saucepan and bring the water to the boil. Reduce the heat and simmer for about 45 minutes, until the barley is tender, topping up the water if necessary. Add the cooked beans, chickpeas and the short-grain rice, and bring the liquid to the boil again. Reduce the heat and simmer for about 15 minutes.

Meanwhile, place all the dried fruit in a bowl and cover with boiling water. Leave to soak for 10 minutes, then drain. Add the fruit to the pan and stir in the sugar. Continue to simmer, stirring from time to time, until the mixture begins to thicken.

Add 2 tablespoons of the hot liquid to the cornflour/corn starch paste and tip it into the pan, stirring all the time. Add the rose water and continue to simmer for another 15 minutes, stirring from time to time, until the mixture is very thick.

Tip the mixture into a large serving bowl. Shake the bowl to make sure the surface is flat and leave the pudding to cool.

To garnish, arrange the dried fruit over the top in a neat pattern around the edge and in the middle, scatter the pine nuts and pomegranate seeds over the surface, before sprinkling with the desiccated coconut. Serve chilled or at room temperature.

The rituals of tea

It could be said that the preparation and drinking of tea is a national pastime in Iran, Turkey and Morocco, where it is regarded as the drink of friendship and hospitality and is offered anywhere at any time of day — in the market, at the bank, in a traffic jam, when conducting business, while travelling by boat or bus and in the family home. On the whole, tea doesn't quite share the same stage as coffee in parts of Saudi Arabia, the Gulf States and Yemen.

Tea, in its dried-leaf form, is thought to have first arrived in the Middle East with the early Persian caravans. However, it didn't make an impact on the collective culinary culture until relatively recently, as coffee was regarded as the beverage of choice and coffee houses were already established as the focal point of many communities. Coffee drinking was banned in Iran in the 1920s after years of suspicion that coffee houses were harbouring groups of political and religious dissent, as well as acts of vice. To replace coffee, new types of tea were imported from China and a culture of tea drinking was encouraged, which filtered through to Turkey. Tea plantations are now a common sight at the eastern end of the Black Sea coast in Turkey and in the Caspian littoral in Iran. Caspian tea is fragrant and expensive and the finest variety is drunk solely in Iran, whereas the Black Sea tea is consumed with gusto in Turkey but is also exported for blends.

Traditionally tea was prepared in samovars, which were imported from Russia. These elaborate vessels were often made of brass with one compartment at the bottom for burning coals to heat up the water in the kettle section, on top of which sat a small teapot brewing tea all day long. These samovars are still in use, particularly in traditional teas houses and tea gardens, but many people have converted to the modern version of a large aluminium teapot, which is filled with water and acts as the kettle for a smaller aluminium teapot placed on top and in which sits the tea. The idea is that the tea can continue to brew over the simmering kettle and be continuously topped up with water and refreshed with new tea leaves as it is drunk, so that one teapot system keeps going over a long period of time.

Generally, tea is served in small, thin glasses, some ornately decorated with silver or gold rims. In formal situations, they can be placed into intricately designed glass-holders fashioned from silver, gold, ivory or tortoise shell. In Morocco, the glasses are often coloured and decorated with Arabic writing or the symbolic Hand of Fatma. The Turkish tea glasses are tulip-shaped, a legacy of one of the Ottoman sultans who fell in love with the shape of the tulip and encouraged its design on tiles, plates and other artefacts. The fragrance and colour of the brew is of importance too, particularly in Iran where the sight of light amber tea in a delicate clear glass is a vision of perfection. For formal entertaining, Iranians sometimes flavour the tea with cinnamon sticks and sprinkle rose petals into the glasses. Milk is never added to traditional tea and sugar lumps are served separately with black tea — in the same fashion as coffee drinking, many locals hold the sugar lump in their teeth and suck the hot tea through it. Herbal teas and Moroccan mint tea, on the other hand, are often sweetened during brewing, which enhances the flavours and aromas of the herbs.

Aromatic infusions and herbal teas are popular throughout the Middle East, utilizing local herbs, spices, barks, leaves and flowers. Ginger, aniseed, cinnamon and cloves are common spices employed in sweet, honey-laced infusions as pick-me-ups and cold remedies; geranium leaves, linden and lime leaves, mint and sage are all brewed as herbal remedies for relaxation, indigestion, coughs and colds; dried pomegranate flowers and dried hibiscus are infused to relieve intestinal complaints and, along with thyme, are reputed to have aphrodisiacal qualities; and fresh, sweetly perfumed orange blossoms or rose petals are added to infusions prepared with scented waters and served on special occasions.

RITUALS OF MOROCCAN TEA

In Morocco, the preparation of mint tea is regarded as a 'gift of God'. There is an element of mystique and ritual involved as it is open to personal interpretation — the variety of mint leaves; the addition of lemon verbena, lemon balm, sage or orange peel; the sweetening with honey or raw sugar; and the pouring and presentation. Often, a spoonful of green tea goes into the pot first, followed by a huge handful of fresh mint leaves and their stalks, literally stuffed in to fill the pot, sugar is added and the boiling water is poured over. The pot is placed over a gentle heat to brew, or it is left to infuse, before it is served with a flourish by holding the pot close to the glass and raising it higher and higher to create a little of the desired bubbly froth on top of each glass.

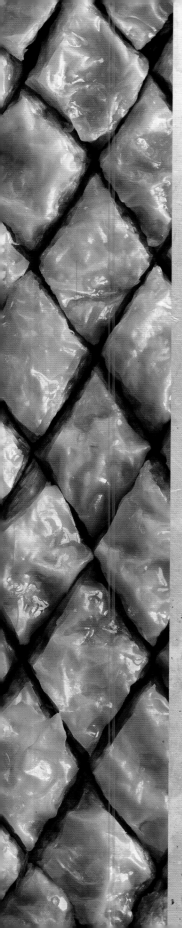

Baklava with pistachios and rose syrup

The grandest of all sweet pastries in the Middle East, baklava is a legacy of the Ottoman Empire. The classic baklava is made with eight layers of specially prepared pastry dough brushed with clarified butter and seven layers of chopped walnut, soaked in a lemon flavoured syrup or honey. The secret is in the dough, which must be made from the finest flour and paper-thin, but many modern versions of baklava are prepared with sheets of 'fila' (filo/phyllo) pastry, which is easy to find and simple to use. Served at any time of day — a mid-morning sweet snack with a cup of strong Turkish coffee, a mid-afternoon pick-me-up with a glass of tea, a late-night treat at the pastry shop — it is also the preferred sweet pastry to bear as a gift when visiting family or friends, or to serve at circumcision and wedding feasts. It is also prepared for religious and national celebrations. The fillings for baklava can vary from a mixture of chopped nuts to a moist, creamy almond paste or a delicately flavoured pumpkin purée. The syrup can be flavoured with lemon juice, orange blossom water or rose water.

175 g/¾ cup clarified or plain butter

100 ml/a scant ½ cup sunflower oil

500 g/1 lb. 2 oz. filo/phyllo pastry sheets, thawed if frozen

450 g/1 lb. unsalted pistachio kernels (or a mixture of almonds, walnuts and pistachios) finely chopped

1 teaspoon ground cinnamon

FOR THE SYRUP

500 g/1 lb. 2 oz. granulated sugar

250 ml/1 cup water

freshly squeezed juice of 1 unwaxed lemon

2–3 tablespoons rose water

a 30-cm/12-in. square baking pan

Serves 8

Preheat the oven to 160°C (325°F) Gas 3.

In a small pan, melt the butter with the oil. Brush a little of it on the base and sides of the baking pan. Place a sheet of filo/phyllo in the bottom and brush it with the melted butter and oil. Continue with half the quantity of filo/phyllo sheets, making sure each one is brushed with the butter and oil. Ease the sheets into the corners and trim the edges if they flop over the rim.

Once you have brushed the last of that batch of filo/phyllo sheets, spread the pistachios over the top and sprinkle with the cinnamon. Then continue as before, layering the remaining filo/phyllo sheets while brushing them with the butter and oil. Brush the top one as well then, using a sharp knife, cut diagonal parallel lines right through all the layers to the bottom to form small diamond shaped portions. Pop the baklava into the preheated oven for about 1 hour, until the top is golden — if the top is still pale, turn the oven up for a few minutes at the end.

Meanwhile, make the syrup. Put the sugar and water into a heavy-based pan. Bring the liquid to the boil, stirring all the time, until the sugar dissolves. Reduce the heat and add the lemon juice and rose water, and simmer for about 15 minutes, until it thickens a little. Leave the syrup to cool in the pan.

When the baklava is ready, remove it from the oven and slowly pour the cold syrup over the piping hot pastry. Put the baklava back into the oven for 2–3 minutes, so that it soaks up the syrup, then take it out and leave it to cool. Once cooled, lift the diamond-shaped pieces of baklava out of the pan and arrange them on a serving dish. Serve with traditional Moroccan mint tea.

Little cakes with mahlab and walnuts

These little Arab cakes, 'ma'amoul' (the Jewish name is 'menena'), are a great family favourite in the Middle East. Prepared in batches and stored in airtight containers, they are commonly stuffed with walnuts or a date paste but for special occasions they are sometimes stuffed with the more expensive and prestigious pistachio nuts. For many Christians, Easter would not be complete without a tray full of freshly baked ma'amoul and the same applies to Muslims at Ramadan, the month of fasting, and Eid al-Fitr, the three day holiday of feasting and celebrating to end the month of fasting. There is a fair amount of competition in the making of a perfect batch of ma'amoul, which can vary in shape and size but should be delicately perfumed or flavoured and simply melt in the mouth as you help yourself to more!

500 g/4 cups plain/all-purpose flour

2 teaspoons mahlab (aromatic spice made from the ground seeds of St Lucie cherries)

225 g/2 sticks salted butter

2 tablespoons icing/confectioners' sugar, plus extra for dusting

2 tablespoons rose water

4—5 tablespoons whole milk

FOR THE FILLING

350 g/2⅓ cups walnuts, finely chopped

1 tablespoons granulated sugar

2 teaspoons ground cinnamon

baking sheet, lightly oiled

Serves 6—8

Preheat the oven to 180°C (350°F) Gas 4.

Sift the flour and mahlab into a bowl. Rub the butter into the flour until it resembles fine breadcrumbs. Sift in the icing/confectioners' sugar and bind with the rose water and milk to form a soft, malleable dough.

Put the filling ingredients into a bowl and mix together well. Take a small apricot-size lump of dough in your fingers and mould it into a ball. Carefully, hollow out the ball to form a deep cavity into which you spoon a little of the nut filling. Fold the edges over the filling, pinch the top to seal it and gently mould the ball in the palm of your hand.

Place the ball on the baking sheet and press it down gently with the palm of your hand. Repeat with the rest of the dough and the filling until you have roughly 30—40 little cakes, depending on their size. Prick the tops with a fork and bake them in the preheated oven for 20—25 minutes, until pale brown but still slightly soft.

Leave the cakes to cool and firm up on the baking sheet, dust them with a little icing/confectioners' sugar, then place them on a serving plate.

Hot milk with orchid root and cinnamon

In the winter, particularly in the cold mountain air, people stop at tea houses and coffee shops to warm up with a cup of thick, milky 'sahlab' ('salep' in Turkish), a hot drink that takes its name from the ground orchid roots used to thicken it. Dried orchid roots, ground to a fine powder, have been used since medieval times as a gelatinous thickening agent, particularly in Turkey, Iran, Syria and Lebanon where it is used for this drink as well as in the preparation of the traditional snowy, white ice cream which is unique to that region because of its unusual elasticity – when it is spooned out it stretches like melted mozzarella. The small, dried orchid roots are threaded onto strings and sold like long beaded necklaces in the markets but you can buy ground dried orchid root (a little goes a long way), or sachets of instant sahlab/salep in Middle Eastern stores.

1 tablespoon ground orchid root or
sahlab/salep

600 ml/2½ cups whole milk

2 tablespoons granulated sugar

1–2 teaspoons ground cinnamon

Serves 4

In a small bowl, slake the ground orchid root or sahlab/salep with a little of the milk to form a loose paste.

Heat the rest of the milk with the sugar in a saucepan, stirring until the sugar has dissolved. Bring the milk to scalding point then spoon a little into the orchid root or sahlab/salep paste and tip the whole mixture back into the scalding milk. Stir vigorously or beat with a balloon whisk, to make sure the orchid root or sahlab/salep doesn't form into little lumps, and keep stirring until the mixture thickens.

Pour the thickened milk into individual cups, dust each one with cinnamon and drink while it is piping hot. Serve with dried dates.

Cherry sherbet

Derived from the word 'sharab', the Arabic word for 'drink', sherbet drinks have a regal status in the Middle East, as they cover a spectrum of flavoured soft drinks in a region with restrictions on alcohol consumption amongst some religious communities. Fruity or floral, the drinks are simply prepared by pouring a fragrant syrup over ice and adding water — the flavour of the syrups vary from delicate ingredients like rose petals to the more robust lemons, limes and cherries.

500 g/1 lb. 2 oz. fresh sour/tart cherries, washed and stoned/pitted

1 kg/5 cups granulated sugar

250 ml/1 cup water

muslin/cheesecloth

sterilized jars or bottles

Put the cherries in a wide, heavy-based pan and cover with the sugar. Leave for at least 2 hours so that the juice weeps into the sugar.

Pour the water into the pot and bring it to the boil, stirring the cherries and sugar all the time. Reduce the heat and simmer gently for 10–15 minutes.

Strain the cherries through a fine-meshed sieve/strainer or a piece of muslin/cheesecloth over a bowl, pressing all the flavour and juice out of the cherries, and return the liquid to the pan. Bring the liquid to the boil and keep it boiling gently until it is thick and syrupy.

Let the syrup cool and pour it into sterilized jars or bottles and store it in a cool place or the refrigerator for 1–2 months. To serve, pour roughly 2 tablespoons syrup over ice and top up the glass with water to taste.

Index

ONLINE SOURCES FOR MIDDLE EASTERN INGREDIENTS

www.melburyandappleton.co.uk
Middle Eastern and North African foods
www.kalama.com
Fresh breads, spices, dried fruit, grains, nuts, teas, coffees and prepared Persian specialties
http://kalustyans.com/
4,000 varieties of spices, herbs, oils, nuts, fruits, coffee, tea and healthy snacks
www.penzeys.com
Online and retail spice and herb emporiums
www.sadaf.com
Mediterranean and Middle Eastern gourmet foods
www.zamourispices.com
Tagines, Moroccan herbs and spices, argan oil, coffee, tea and more

PICTURE CREDITS

acknowledgements

My passion for Middle Eastern food is as boundless as the hospitality I receive when travelling in the region and for that I have thanked many friends and strangers and will continue to do so every time I return. When it comes to the production of this book, I would like to thank Julia Charles for commissioning it in the first place and for all her support along the way; Rebecca Woods for her enthusiasm at the beginning of the project and Nathan Joyce for stepping into her shoes so smoothly and with such charm; and finally to Steve Painter who, along with his talented food styling team, Lucy McKelvie and her assistant, Ellie Jarvis, has managed to capture the atmosphere of the wide-reaching culinary culture with his beautiful photography and design.